Berlitz® speaking your language

P9-CDK-614

French
in 30 days

Course Book
by Micheline Funke

French
in 30 days
Course Book
by Micheline Funke

Berlitz Publishing
New York   London   Singapore

Contacting the Editors
Every effort has been made to provide accurate information in this publication, but changes are inevitable. The publisher cannot be responsible for any resulting loss, inconvenience or injury. We would appreciate it if readers would call our attention to any errors or outdated information. Please contact us at: comments@berlitzpublishing.com

Original edition: 2001 by Langenscheidt KG, Berlin and Munich

Second edition: 2014
Printed in China

Berlitz Trademark Reg. U.S. Patent Office and other countries. Marca Registrada.
Used under license from Berlitz Investment Corporation

Senior Commissioning Editor: Kate Drynan
Design: Beverley Speight
Picture research: Beverley Speight

Cover photos: © from left to right, Ilpo Musto, 1, 5, 7; Kevin Cummins 2, 3, 4, 6, 8
Interior photos: © istockphotos p22, 44, 64, 91, 110, 117, 125, 134, 159, 169, 177, 188, 194, 202, 217, 233, 239,251; APA Ilpo Musto p28; APA K Cummins p72, 82, 153; APA Bev Speight p54, 146; APA Sylvaine Pointau p36, 102, 226; APA Greg Gladman p210; APA Peter Stuckings p15, 245.

Distribution

Worldwide
APA Publications GmbH & Co. Verlag KG
(Singapore branch)
7030 Ang Mo Kio Ave 5
08-65 Northstar @ AMK, Singapore 569880
Email: apasin@singnet.com.sg

US
Ingram Publisher Services
One Ingram Blvd, PO Box 3006
La Vergne, TN 37086-1986
Email: ips@ingramcontent.com

UK and Ireland
Dorling Kindersley Ltd
(a Penguin Company)
80 Strand, London, WC2R ORL, UK
Email: sales@uk.dk.com

Australia
Woodslane
10 Apollo St
Warriewood, NSW 2102
Email: info@woodslane.com.au

Contents

How to Use this Book		6
Pronunciation		7
Quick Reference		11
The Alphabet, Numbers, Days, Months		12
Day 1	*At the station*	15
Day 2	*Dining In*	22
Day 3	*Welcome to Paris*	28
Day 4	*Shopping*	35
Day 5	*The family*	44
Test 1		**52**
Day 6	*Education*	54
Day 7	*Making friends*	63
Day 8	*Sightseeing*	72
Day 9	*Café culture*	82
Day 10	*Shopping*	91

Test 2		100
Day 11	*Dining out*	102
Day 12	*At the station*	110
Day 13	*The ski trip*	117
Day 14	*A chance encounter*	125
Day 15	*Making calls*	134

Test 3		144
Day 16	*Work experience*	146
Day 17	*The internship*	153
Day 18	*Going out*	159
Day 19	*Celebrations*	169
Day 20	*Driving in France*	177

Test 4		186
Day 21	*The breakdown*	188
Day 22	*At the doctor's*	195
Day 23	*Camping*	202
Day 24	*Markets*	210
Day 25	*Making plans*	217

Test 5	224

Day 26	*At the beach*	226
Day 27	*The meeting*	233
Day 28	*Finding work*	239
Day 29	*Goodbye*	245
Day 30	*Keeping in touch*	251

Country and culture quiz	260
Key to the exercises	262
Vocabulary refresher	273

How to Use this Book

French in 30 Days is a self-study course which will provide you with a basic knowledge of everyday French in a very short time. The course is divided into 30 short, manageable daily lessons. This book will familiarize you with the main grammatical structures of French and provide you with a good command of essential vocabulary. In 30 days you will acquire both an active and a passive understanding of the language, enabling you to function effectively in day-to-day life.

Each chapter is an episode in a journey that takes place over 30 days, from your arrival to your final departure, with the main focus on typical, day-to-day situations. Each day has the same pattern: first, there is a short intro into what you will learn as well as some country and culture information about France. You will then have a text in French – generally a dialogue – followed by a grammar section and a number of exercises to help reinforce what you have learned. At the end of each lesson you will find a list of vocabulary. The quick grammar and vocabulary tests, together with the answer key at the back of the book, will enable you to check your progress.

The audio CD contains all the dialogues from the book. These are marked by a CD symbol. Days 1 to 10 are spoken twice: the first time, quickly and fluently so that you get used to hearing everyday French and, the second time, slowly and more clearly. From day 11 onwards you'll be advanced enough to follow the French text, which will now be spoken only once, in the faster speech of everyday language.

Pronunciation

Consonants

Letter	Approximate pronunciation	Example
ch	like *sh* in shut	**chercher**
ç	like *s* in sit	**ça**
g	1) before *e*, *i*, *y*, like *s* in pleasure	**manger**
	2)before *a*, *o*, *u*, like *g* in go	**garçon**
gn	like *ni* in onion	**ligne**
h	always silent	**homme**
j	like *s* in pleasure	**jamais**
qu	like *k* in kill	**qui**
r	rolled in the back of the mouth, rather like gargling	**rouge**
w	usually like *v* in voice	**wagon**

Vowels

Letter	Approximate pronunciation	Example
a, à, â	between the *a* in hat and the *a* in father	**mari**
é or **ez**	like *a* in late	**été**
è, ê, e	like *e* in get	**même**
e	sometimes like *er* in other	**je**
i	like *ee* in meet	**il**
o	generally like *o* in hot but sometimes like *oa* in soar	**donner**
		rose
ô	like *oa* in soar	**Rhône**
u	like *ew* in dew	**cru**

Letters *b*, *c*, *d*, *f*, *k*, *l*, *m*, *n*, *p*, *s*, *t*, *v*, *x* and *z* are pronounced as in English.

Sounds spelled with two or more letters

Letters	Approximate pronunciation	Example
ai, aient, ay	like *a* in late	**j'ai**
ais, ait	or	**vais**
aî, ei	like *e* in get	**chaîne**
		peine
(e)au	similar to *oa* in soar	**chaud**
eu, eû,	like *u* in fur, but with lips rounded	**peu**
œu	like a puff of air	
euil, euille	like *uh* in huh, but without pronouncing the *h* and with a *y* sound added	**feuille**
ail, aille	like *ie* in tie	**taille**
oi, oy	like *w* followed by the *a* in hat	**moi**
ou, oû	like *o* in move or *oo* in hoot	**nouveau**
ui	like *wee* in between	**traduire**

Nasal sounds

French contains nasal vowels. A nasal vowel is pronounced simultaneously through the mouth and the nose.

Letters	Approximate pronunciation	Example
am, an	something like *arn* in tarnish	**tante**
em, en	generally like the previous sound	**entrée**
ien	sounds like *yan* in yank	**bien**
im, in, aim, ain, eim, ein	approximately like *ang* in rang	**instant**
om, on	approximately like *ong* in song	**maison**
um, un	approximately like *ang* in rang	**brun**

Liaison and Stress

Normally, final consonants of words are not pronounced in French. However, when a word ending in a consonant is followed by one beginning with a vowel, they are often run together, and the consonant is pronounced as if it began the following word.

All syllables in French are pronounced with more or less the same degree of stress (loudness).

The Alphabet

The French alphabet is the same as English, although the letter **w** appears only in foreign words. It also uses several accents: **grave** (`` ` ``), **acute** (´), **circumflex** (^) and the **cedilla** (**ç** - only on the letter **c**).

A	ah		**T**	tay
B	bay		**U**	ew
C	say		**V**	fay
D	day		**W**	doobleh-vey
E	eh		**X**	eeks
F	ef		**Y**	ee grehk
G	zhay		**Z**	zed
H	ahsh			
I	ee			
J	zhee			
K	kah			
L	el			
M	em			
N	en			
O	o			
P	pay			
Q	kew			
R	ehr			
S	ess			

Numbers

0	**zéro** *zay·roh*
1	**un** *uhN*
2	**deux** *duh*
3	**trois** *trwah*
4	**quatre** *kah·truh*
5	**cinq** *sehNk*
6	**six** *sees*
7	**sept** *seht*
8	**huit** *weet*
9	**neuf** *nuhf*
10	**dix** *dees*
11	**onze** *ohNz*
12	**douze** *dooz*
13	**treize** *trehz*
14	**quatorze** *kah·tohrz*
15	**quinze** *kehNz*
16	**seize** *sehz*
17	**dix-sept** *dee·seht*
18	**dix-huit** *deez·weet*
19	**dix-neuf** *deez·nuhf*
20	**vingt** *vehN*
21	**vingt-et-un** *vehN·tay·uhN*
22	**vingt-deux** *vehN·duh*

30	**trente** *trawNt*
31	**trente-et-un** *trawN•tay•uhN*
40	**quarante** *kah•rawNt*
50	**cinquante** *sehN•kawNt*
60	**soixante** *swah•zawNt*
70	**soixante-dix** *swah•zawNt•dees*
80	**quatre-vingt** *kah•truh•vehN*
90	**quatre-vingt-dix** *kah•truh•vehN•dees*
100	**cent** *sawN*
101	**cent-un** *sawN•uhN*
200	**deux-cent** *duh•sawN*
500	**cinq-cent** *sehNk•sawN*
1,000	**mille** *meel*
10,000	**dix mille** *dee meel*
1,000,000	**un million** *uhN meel•yohN*

Days

Monday	**lundi** *luhN·dee*
Tuesday	**mardi** *mahr·dee*
Wednesday	**mercredi** *mehr·kruh·dee*
Thursday	**jeudi** *zhuh·dee*
Friday	**vendredi** *vawN·druh·dee*
Saturday	**samedi** *sahm·dee*
Sunday	**dimanche** *dee·mawNsh*

Months

January	**janvier** *zhawN·veeyay*
February	**février** *fay·vreeyay*
March	**mars** *mahrs*
April	**avril** *ah·vreel*
May	**mai** *may*
June	**juin** *zhwehN*
July	**juillet** *zhwee·yay*
August	**août** *oot*
September	**septembre** *sehp·tawN·bruh*
October	**octobre** *ohk·toh·bruh*
November	**novembre** *noh·vawN·bruh*
December	**décembre** *day·sawN·bruh*

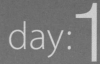

At the station

Welcome to France! Day 1 marks your arrival in France. You will learn how to form the present tense of regular verbs ending in *-er*, the present tense of verbs *être* (to be) and *avoir* (to have), personal pronouns (I, you, he, etc). You will also start to build your vocabulary, and pick up some important language and cultural tips.

BONJOUR...

*To say hello in France, you can simply say **Bonjour Monsieur** (Mr) /**Madame** (Mrs) /**Mademoiselle** (Miss) or **Bonjour Michel/Claire**. **Bonjour** is an informal greeting that can be used all day. In the evening you can say **Bonsoir** to mean both hello and goodbye. **Au revoir** is the formal word for goodbye. **Salut !** meaning Hello!/Hi! (as well as Cheers! when clinking glasses for a toast) is another informal option that can be used on its own.*

French conversation: Accueil à la gare de l'Est

A Paris.

Michel:	Bonjour Mademoiselle, vous êtes bien Mademoiselle Dietz ?
Claire:	Oui, c'est moi, vous êtes Monsieur Rougier ?
Michel:	Oui, je m'appelle Michel.
Claire:	Et moi, c'est Claire.
Michel:	Vous avez des bagages ?
Claire:	J'ai juste un sac et une valise.
Michel:	Donnez-moi tout ça. Je suis en voiture, la voiture est garée rue de Chabrol, c'est tout près.

Arrivée chez les Rougier.

Michel:	Caroline, je te présente Mademoiselle Dietz.
Caroline:	Bienvenue.
Claire:	Bonjour Madame.
Caroline:	Pas Madame, Caroline. Les enfants, ...

Les enfants arrivent.

Florent, Annick, Julie:	Salut !
Claire:	Bonjour, les enfants !
Florent:	Moi, je m'appelle Florent.
Annick:	Moi, je m'appelle Annick.
Claire:	Et toi ?
Julie:	Moi, c'est Julie. Les fleurs, c'est pour toi.
Claire:	Merci, c'est gentil !

English conversation: Meeting at gare de l'Est

In Paris.

Michel:	Excuse me, are you Ms. Dietz?
Claire:	Yes, I am, and you are Mr. Rougier?
Michel:	Yes, that's right, my name is Michel.
Claire:	And I am Claire.
Michel:	Do you have any luggage?
Claire:	I just have a bag and one suitcase.
Michel:	Give them to me. I've got my car here. It is parked on rue de Chabrol, which is just around the corner.

Arrival at the Rougier family's home.

Michel:	Caroline, let me introduce you to Ms. Dietz.

Caroline:	Welcome!
Claire:	Hello Mrs. Rougier.
Caroline:	Don't call me Mrs. Rougier. Call me Caroline. Children, ...
The children arrive.	
Florent, Annick, Julie:	Hello!
Claire:	Hello!
Florent:	My name is Florent.
Annick:	My name is Annick.
Claire:	And what's yours?
Julie:	I'm Julie, and the flowers are for you!
Claire:	Thank you. That's nice of you!

Grammar

Present tense

Below is the present tense of the irregular verbs **être** (to be) and **avoir** (to have). You need to learn these!

être	to be	avoir	to have
je suis	I am	j'ai	I have
tu es	you are	tu as	you have
il/elle est	he/she is	il/elle a	he/she/it has
nous sommes	we are	nous avons	we have
vous êtes	you are	vous avez	you have
ils/elles sont	they are	ils/elles ont	they have

Personal pronouns

singular		plural	
je, j'	I	nous	we
tu	you	vous	you
il	he	ils	they *(masc.)*
elle	she	elles	they *(fem.)*
vous	you		

Before **vowels** and silent **h**, replace **je** with **j'** (j'ai).
Use **vous** instead of **tu** as a more formal and polite form.
il can also be used as an impersonal pronoun to mean *it*:

il est 2 heures	it is 2 o'clock

Vous or *tu*?

When addressing people, the French distinguish between the formal **vous** (you formal or plural) and the more familiar and informal address **tu** (you singular). **Tu** is used among family and relatives, close friends, children and young people. **Vous** is appropriate when meeting someone new, for addressing strangers (for example shop assistants), adults, and in official situations.

Definite and indefinite article

In French all nouns are either masculine or feminine and take either **le** (masculine), **la** (feminine) or **les** (masculine or feminine plural).

singular			
masculine	*feminine*	*masculine*	*feminine*
le sac	la gare	un sac	une gare

Note that for nouns beginning with a vowel or what is known as a **silent h** (because in French the letter **h** is not pronounced), **l'** replaces the **le/la**
l'hotel *m* (the hotel)
l'arrivée *f* (the arrival)

Unlike English, French also has a **plural form** of the indefinite article (the):

plural			
masculine	*feminine*	*masculine*	*feminine*
les sacs	les gares	des sacs	des gares

un sac (a bag) /**des sacs** (bags)
une gare (a station) / **des gares** (stations)

Present tense - verbs ending in *-er*

To form the present tense of verbs ending in **-er**, you simply **drop the -er** and replace by the endings in the table below. The verb **arriver** (to arrive) is given as an example.

	ending	arriver (to arrive)
je/j' ...	-e	j'arrive
tu ...	-es	tu arrives
il/elle ...	-e	il/elle arrive
nous	-ons	nous arrivons
vous ...	-ez	vous arrivez
ils/elles ...	-ent	ils/elles arrivent

Disjunctive personal pronouns

	singular	plural
1st person	moi	nous
2nd person	toi	vous
3rd person	lui *(masculine)*	eux *(masculine)*
	elle *(feminine)*	elles *(feminine)*

Moi and toi can be used alone (i.e. without a verb) for emphasis:

Moi, je m'appelle Florent.	My name is Florent, I am Florent.

After c'est:

C'est toi?	Is it you?	Oui, c'est moi.	Yes, it's me.

After a preposition:

Les fleurs, c'est pour toi !	The flowers are for you!

Exercises

Exercise 1

Fill in the correct form of the verb in brackets below.

1 Claire et Monsieur Rougier (être) .... à la gare de l'Est.

2 Vous (être) .... Mademoiselle Dietz ?

3 Oui, c'(être) .... moi.

4 Vous (avoir) .... des bagages ?

5 J'(avoir) .... une valise.

6 Vous (être) .... gentil !

7 Je (être) .... en voiture.

8 La voiture (être) .... rue de Chabrol.

9 Monsieur et Madame Rougier (avoir) .... 3 enfants.

10 Julie (avoir) .... des fleurs pour Claire.

Exercise 2

Follow the example and fill in **il** or **elle** as appropriate.

(Claire) a une valise.   **Elle a une valise.**

1 (Monsieur Rougier) .... est à la gare.

2 (Claire) .... est à la gare.

3 (Monsieur Rougier) .... a une voiture.

4 (Claire) .... a des bagages.

Exercise 3

Fill in the correct form of the verb in brackets.

1 Claire (arriver) .... chez les Rougier.

2 Michel Rougier (présenter) .... Claire à Caroline.

3 Je te (présenter) .... Claire.

4 Florent, Annick et Julie (arriver) ....

Exercise 4

Match the questions to the answers.

a Bonjour, Mademoiselle, vous êtes bien Mademoiselle Dietz ?

b Vous êtes Monsieur Rougier ?

c Les enfants, je vous présente Claire !

d Je m'appelle Claire et toi ?

1 Oui, je m'appelle Michel.

2 Salut, Claire !

3 Moi, je m'appelle Annick.

4 Oui, c'est moi.

A ....   **B**...............................   **C** ....   **D**...............................

Exercise 5

What do you say if you ... Match the answers in French below to each question.

1 ... want to introduce yourself?

2 ... want to make sure that you have addressed the right person?

3 ... were correctly addressed?

4 ... want to introduce a friend to someone else?

a Je te présente ...

b Oui, c'est moi ...

c Vous êtes bien ...

d Je m'appelle ... *or*: Je suis ...

1 .... 2 .... 3 .... 4 ....

Vocabulary

Below is a list of vocabulary encountered in this chapter.

accueil *m*	*reception/welcome*	**je te présente**	*let me introduce you to*
arrivée *f*	*arrival*	**la voiture est**	*the car is parked*
arriver	*to arrive*	**garée**	
bagages *m pl*	*luggage/ bags*	**Madame** *f*	*Mrs./Ms.*
bienvenue *f*	*welcome*	**Mademoiselle** *f*	*Miss/Ms.*
bonjour	*hello*	**Monsieur** *m*	*Mr.*
c'est gentil	*that's nice*	**pour**	*for*
c'est moi	*that's me*	**présenter**	*to introduce*
chez les Rougier	*at the Rougier's (house)*	**rue** *f*	*street*
enfant *m*	*child*	**sac** *m*	*bag*
est (être)	*is (to be)*	**salut**	*hi*
Et toi?	*And you?*	**tout près**	*nearby/ just here*
gare *f*	*station*	**valise** *f*	*suitcase*
je m'appelle	*my name is (to call*	**voiture** *f*	*car*
(s'appeler)	*oneself)*	**vous êtes (être)**	*you are (to be)*
je suis (être)	*I am (to be)*		

Dining in

Day 2 introduces the present tense of the irregular verbs *faire* (to do/make) and *aller* (to go). You will learn how French sentences are formed and how to make plurals, and you will discover more about French culture.

EATING HABITS...

*A standard French breakfast (**petit déjeuner**) at home will usually include coffee, tea hot chocolate, bread or toast, butter and jam.*

*During the day the French usually have two meals; at lunchtime they have **le déjeuner** and in the evening **le dîner**. Lunch for the working population can often be a hot meal from a **traiteur** (a caterer that provides cooked takeaway meals) or a slice of quiche or a salad or sandwich from a local **boulangerie** (bakery). The evening meal rarely takes place before 8:00 p.m.*

French conversation: Premier dîner en famille

Caroline:	Ce soir, il y a de la soupe, une omelette et de la salade verte, après du fromage ou des yaourts, j'ai aussi des fruits. Vous avez faim ?
Claire:	Oui, mais j'ai surtout soif.
Caroline:	Vous voulez du jus de fruit, de l'eau minérale, du vin, de la bière ?
Claire:	Pour moi, juste un verre d'eau, s'il vous plaît.
Caroline:	Vous aimez la soupe ?
Claire:	Oh oui, beaucoup.
Caroline:	Vous faites du ski alpin ou du ski de fond ?
Claire:	Je préfère le ski alpin.
Florent:	Tu fais d'autres sports ?
Claire:	En été, je fais de la randonnée, je vais nager à la piscine.
Caroline:	Nous aimons aussi la randonnée mais plutôt en automne dans les forêts des environs de Paris.
Claire:	Et toi, Annick, qu'est-ce que tu aimes faire comme sport ?
Annick:	Moi, j'aime bien faire du vélo à la campagne en été. Je vais souvent à la piscine.
Claire:	Et toi, Julie, tu aimes aussi aller à la piscine ?
Julie:	Oui, moi, je sais nager depuis les dernières vacances en Bretagne !

English conversation: First dinner with the family

Caroline:	Tonight we're having soup, an omelet and a green salad, followed by cheese or yogurt, and I also have fruit. Are you hungry?
Claire:	Yes, but mostly I'm thirsty.
Caroline:	What would you like to drink, fruit juice, mineral water, wine, beer?
Claire:	Just a glass of water for me, please.
Caroline:	Do you like soup?
Claire:	Oh yes, very much.
Caroline:	Do you go downhill skiing or cross-country?
Claire:	I prefer downhill.
Florent:	Do you do any other sports?
Claire:	In the summer I go hiking or swim in the swimming pool.
Caroline:	We like hiking too, but mostly in the autumn in the forests around Paris.
Claire:	What about you, Annick, what types of sport do you like?

Annick:	I like cycling in the country in the summer. I often go to the swimming pool.
Claire:	And what about you, Julie, do you like going to the swimming pool, too?
Julie:	Yes, I can swim since our last holiday in Brittany!

Grammar

Present tense of *faire* and *aller*

Faire and **aller** are both irregular verbs. You will need to learn these by heart.

faire to make/do	aller to go
je fais	je vais
tu fais	tu vas
il/elle fait	il/elle va
nous faisons	nous allons
vous faites	vous allez
ils/elles font	ils/elles vont

The partitive article: *du, de la, de l'*

masculine	
du (de + le)	de l' (in front of a vowel or silent h)
du café (coffee)	de l'argent (money)

feminine	
de la	
de la salade (salad)	de l'eau (water)

Note: English has no equivalent for the partitive article.
Du, de la, de l' designate an indefinable quantity.

Vous voulez de l'eau?	Would you like some water?
J'ai du café.	I'm having coffee.

For a precise specification of a quantity, de or d' in front of a vowel or silent h is used, e.g. un verre de vin, a glass of wine; un verre de bière, a glass of beer; un verre d'eau, a glass of water, i.e. without the article of the noun it refers to.

The partitive article is also used in a number of standing expressions, e.g. faire du vélo (riding a bicycle); faire du sport (playing sport).

Plurals

Generally, the plural of nouns is formed by simply adding an -s to the singular form, see below. However, there are some exceptions that end in -aux which you will learn more about in Day 24 on page 213.

singular	plural
le sac	*les* sacs
la valise	*les* valises
un enfant	*des* enfants
un fruit	des fruits
une omelette	*des* omelettes

Exercises

Exercise 1

Fill in the correct form of the verb in brackets.

1 Je (faire) .... du vélo.

2 Elle (aller) .... à la piscine.

3 Ils (faire) .... du sport.

4 Je (aller) .... à York.

5 Il (faire) .... du vélo.

6 Elle (aller) .... faire du ski.

Exercise 2

Fill in du, de la, de l' or des.

Caroline fait .... randonnée. Moi, je fais .... ski, et toi? Moi, je fais .... vélo. Ce soir, il y a

.... fromage, ... fruits, ... salade verte. Vous voulez .... bière?

Exercise 3

Fill in un, une or des.

Il y a .... lacs près de York. Elle a .... voiture. Nous avon .... bagages. Ils ont ....

enfants. Vous avez .... verre?

Exercise 4

Fill in the correct ending for the verbs given.

Elle **aim** .... faire du ski. J'**aim** .... Paris en hiver. Nous **aim** .... nager. Vous **aim** ....

Brahms? Tu **aim** .... faire du vélo? Les enfants **aim** .... les vacances à la campagne.

Vocabulary

Below is a list of vocabulary encountered in this chapter.

à la campagne	*in the country*	juste	*only*
aimer	*to like*	lac *m*	*lake*
avoir faim	*to be hungry*	les dernières	*the last vacation/holiday*
avoir soif	*to be thirsty*	vacances	
beaucoup	*very much, a lot*	nager	*to swim*
bière *f*	*beer*	omelette *f*	*omelet/ omelette*
campagne *f*	*countryside*	parler de	*to speak about*
ce soir	*tonight*	piscine *f*	*swimming pool*
croire	*to believe*	préférer	*to prefer*
depuis	*since*	près de	*close to, near*
dîner *m*	*dinner*	randonnée *f*	*hike*
eau minérale *f*	*mineral water*	savoir	*to know*
en automne	*in the autumn*	salade *f*	*salad*
en Bretagne	*in Brittany*	ski alpin *m*	*downhill skiing*
en été	*in the summer*	ski de fond *m*	*cross-country skiing*
en hiver	*in the winter*	ski *m*	*ski*
faire de la	*to hike*	soir *m*	*evening*
randonnée		soupe *f*	*soup*
faire du ski	*to ski*	sport *m*	*sport*
faire du vélo	*to cycle*	vacances *f pl*	*vacation/holidays*
forêt *f*	*forest*	vélo *m*	*bicycle*
fromage *m*	*cheese*	verre *m*	*glass*
fruit *m*	*fruit*	ville *f*	*city, town*
famille *f*	*family*	vin *m*	*wine*
il y a	*there is*	vouloir	*to want*
jardin *m*	*garden*	yaourt *m*	*yogurt*
jus de fruits *m*	*fruit juice*		

day: 3

Welcome to Paris

Day 3 sees you settling into life in France. You will learn the present tense of a few essential verbs that will make it easy to start conversing in French such as *prendre* (to take) and *vouloir* (to want/wish for). You will also learn how to form basic questions and continue to build your vocabulary.

FRENCH LESSONS...

The Alliance française is a private higher education language school that offers language and country and culture classes in French. Individuals must carry out an assessment before commencing a course in order to assess their level. There are a multitude of courses available for learning French in France so it is best to research the one that best suits your requirements.

French conversation: Première journée à Paris

Petit déjeuner.

Caroline:	Bien dormi ?
Claire:	Très bien, merci !
Caroline:	Servez-vous, il y a du pain, du beurre, de la confiture, des corn-flakes si vous voulez. Vous prenez du café, du thé, du chocolat ?
Claire:	Je prends du thé.
Caroline:	Qu'est-ce que vous faites aujourd'hui ?
Claire:	J'accompagne d'abord Julie à la maternelle et après je passe chercher le programme des cours de langue à l'Alliance française.
Caroline:	C'est tout près de chez nous, mais prenez quand même un plan de Paris.

A l'Alliance française.

Claire:	Bonjour, je voudrais faire un cours intensif de français.
Secrétaire:	Oui, vous avez fait combien d'années de français ?
Claire:	4 ans au lycée.
Secrétaire:	Bien, je vous donne le programme. Vous pouvez choisir un cours. Je vous conseille le niveau moyen ou avancé, de toute façon avant l'inscription, vous devez faire un test.
Claire:	D'accord, les cours commencent quand ?
Secrétaire:	La semaine prochaine. Vous devez remplir ce formulaire.

English conversation: First day in Paris

Breakfast.

Caroline:	Did you sleep well?
Claire:	Very well, thank you.
Caroline:	Help yourself: there is bread, butter, jam or cornflakes if you want. Do you want coffee, tea or hot chocolate?
Claire:	I'll have tea.
Caroline:	What are your plans for today?
Claire:	First, I'll take Julie to kindergarten, and then I'll try to get the program of courses from the Alliance française.
Caroline:	It's very close to us, but you should take a street plan with you all the same.

At Alliance française.

Claire:	Good morning, I would like to enrol in an intensive course in French.

Secretary:	OK. How many years have you been learning French?
Claire:	Four years at high school.
Secretary:	Good, I'll give you the program. You can choose one of the courses. I recommend you attend an intermediate level or advanced level course. In either case, you'll have to pass a test before enrolment.
Claire:	OK, when do classes start?
Secretary:	Next week. You have to fill out this form.

Grammar

Present tense of *prendre* and *vouloir*

Note that prendre is a regular verb and vouloir is irregular.

prendre	to take	vouloir	to want
je prends		je veux	
tu prends		tu veux	
il/elle prend		il/elle veut	
nous prenons		nous voulons	
vous prenez		vous voulez	
ils/elles prennent		ils/elles veulent	

Questions by intonation and the use of *qu'est-ce que*

Vous avez des bagages ?	Do you have any luggage?
Vous êtes monsieur Rougier ?	Are you Mr. Rougier?
Vous voulez de l'eau minérale ?	Would you like mineral water?

In this type of question the word order remains the same as in the statement, but the intonation changes. Note that in French, there is always a space before question marks (and exclamation marks).

statement:	Julie sait nager.	Julie can swim.
question:	Julie sait nager ?	Can Julie swim?
Qu'est-ce que vous faites aujourd'hui ?		What are you doing today?
Qu'est-ce que tu aimes (faire) comme sport ?		What types of sport do you like?

Use qu'est-ce que (what) to ask for a thing. This interrogative clause contains a sub-question, which is confined to one specific piece of information.

Present tense of *devoir* and *pouvoir*

devoir	(to have to, must)	pouvoir	(to be able to, can)
je dois		je peux	
tu dois		tu peux	
il/elle doit		il/elle peut	
nous devons		nous pouvons	
vous devez		vous pouvez	
ils/elles doivent		ils/elles peuvent	

Exercises

Exercise 1

Insert the appropriate form of prendre.

Qu'est-ce que tu .... au petit déjeuner ? Je .... du thé. Caroline ....

du café. Annick et Julie .... du chocolat. Florent .... des corn-flakes.

Nous .... du pain et de la confiture.

Exercise 2

Look at the following example and ask questions using qu'est-ce que.

Qu'est-ce que vous prenez?   Je prends du café

1 .... Je prends du thé.

2 .... J'aime faire du vélo.

3 .... Je veux faire du sport.

4 .... Je fais de la randonnée.

5 .... Je prends de l'eau minérale.

6 .... J'aime la musique classique.

7 .... J'accompagne Julie à la maternelle.

8 .... Je veux faire un cours intensif.

Exercise 3

Fill in the correct form of the verb in brackets.

1 Je (devoir) .... accompagner Julie à la maternelle.

2 Vous (devoir) .... faire un test.

3 Elle (pouvoir) .... passer chercher le programme.

4 Je (pouvoir) .... choisir un cours intensif.

Exercise 4

Qu'est-ce que vous faites aujourd'hui? Match the two columns to form sentences.

1 J'accompagne   **a** nager à la piscine

2 Je passe   **b** chercher le programme des cours

3 Je fais   **c** un cours intensif

4 Je vais   **d** Julie à la maternelle

5 Je dois   **e** faire un test

1.........   2.........   3.........   4.........   5.........

Exercise 5

Something in each line is out of place. What is it?

1 le jus de fruit	la bière	l'eau minérale	le pain
2 le ski	la randonnée	la gare	le sport
3 les fleurs	la confiture	le fromage	la salade
4 le cours	l'inscription	les vacances	le test
5 le lac	la forêt	la ville	le jardin

1.................   2.................   3.................   4.................   5.................

Vocabulary

Below is a list of vocabulary encountered in this chapter.

accompagner	to accompany	**lycée** m	high school
an m	year	**maternelle** f	kindergarten, pre-school
année f	year	**merci**	thank you
après	after(wards)	**niveau avancé** m	advanced level
aujourd'hui	today	**niveau moyen** m	intermediate level
avant	before	**programme** m	program/programme
beurre m	butter	**pain** m	bread
bien	well	**passer chercher**	to pick up
café m	coffee	**plan** m	street plan/map
chocolat m	(hot) chocolate	**pouvoir**	to be able to, can
combien de	how many	**(vous pouvez)**	
commencer	to start	**prendre**	to take
confiture f	jam, marmalade	**Qu'est-ce que?**	What?
cours de	French course	**quand**	when
français m		**quand même**	nevertheless, all the same
cours de	language course	**se servir**	to help oneself
langue m		**(servez-vous)**	(serve yourselves)
cours intensif m	intensive course	**test** m	test
d'abord	first	**thé** m	tea
d'accord	agreed, OK	**tout près de**	very close to us/our house
devoir	to have to, must	**chez nous**	
dormi (dormir)	slept (to sleep)	**vouloir**	to want to
fait (faire)	done (to do)	**(je voudrais,**	(I want to, you (pl.)
inscription f	enrollment/enrolment	**vous voulez)**	want to)
la semaine	next week		
prochaine			

day: 4

Shopping

Day 4 covers numbers and counting. You will learn how to make basic sentences that refer to the past using the perfect tense formed with *avoir* (to have). You will continue to discover more about French country and culture and further improve your vocabulary.

OPENING HOURS...

Food shops, especially bakeries, tend to open early; *boutiques* *and* *les* *grands magasins* *open from 9:00a.m., but sometimes not until 10:00 a.m. In most town centres, just about everything closes from noon until around 2:00 p.m. onwards. However, in Paris and other major cities, some places will stay open. Most shops will close by 7:00p.m. in the evening.* *Hypermarchés* *(usually located on the outskirts of towns), stay open until 8:00 or 9:00p.m. Note that many shops are* *closed* *on* *Mondays.*

French conversation: Courses dans le quartier

Caroline:	Je peux te demander un service ?
Claire:	Bien sûr, de quoi s'agit-il ?
Caroline:	Voilà, j'ai téléphoné à Mamie. Elle est malade. Je vais la voir cet après-midi et avant je passe à la pharmacie pour elle. Il est déjà 11 heures et je n'ai pas le temps de faire les courses. Tu pourrais aller au marché ?
Claire:	Oui, de toute façon je n'ai rien de prévu ce matin. Je dois passer à la poste, le marché est à côté.
Caroline:	Bon, alors prends un kilo de tomates, une salade et des fruits, s'il te plaît.
Claire:	C'est tout ?
Caroline:	Oui, ne m'attends pas pour déjeuner.
Claire:	D'accord, alors à plus tard.
Au marché.	
Marchand:	A qui le tour ?
Claire:	C'est à moi.
Marchand:	Qu'est-ce qu'il vous faut ?
Claire:	Un kilo de tomates à 2,20 euros, s'il vous plaît.
Marchand:	Et avec ça ?
Claire:	Une salade.
Marchand:	Qu'est-ce que vous préférez? Une laitue, une frisée ?
Claire:	Donnez-moi une frisée. Qu'est-ce que vous avez comme pommes aujourd'hui ?
Marchand:	J'ai des golden superbes, pas cher en plus, je vous en mets combien ?
Claire:	Un kilo, s'il vous plaît.
Marchand:	Vous désirez autre chose ?
Claire:	Merci, ça sera tout.
Marchand:	Bon, ça fait 10 euros.

English conversation: Shopping in the neighborhood

Caroline:	Could you do me a favor?
Claire:	Sure, what is it?
Caroline:	Well, I called grandma. She is sick. I'll go and visit her this afternoon and before that I'll have to go to the pharmacy for her. It is already 11 o'clock and I have no time to go shopping. Could you go to the market?
Claire:	Yes, actually, I don't have any more plans for this morning. I'll have to go to the post office and the market is just around the corner.
Caroline:	Good, can you get a kilo of tomatoes, lettuce and some fruit please?
Claire:	Is that all?
Caroline:	Yes. Don't wait for me for lunch.
Claire:	OK. See you later.

At the market.

Merchant:	Who's next?
Claire:	Me.
Merchant:	What would you like?
Claire:	One kilo of tomatoes for 2.20 euros, please.
Merchant:	Anything else?
Claire:	A lettuce.
Merchant:	What do you prefer? A normal green lettuce or a frisee lettuce?
Claire:	Give me the frisee lettuce. What kind of apples do you have today?
Merchant:	I have some wonderful Golden Delicious, at a good price. How many do you want?
Claire:	One kilo.
Merchant:	Would you like anything else?
Claire:	No thanks, that's all.
Merchant:	OK, that'll be 10 euros.

Grammar

Numbers

0	zéro	30	trente	85	quatre-vingt-cinq
1	un/une	31	trente et un(e)	86	quatre-vingt-six
2	deux	32	trente-deux	87	quatre-vingt-sept
3	trois	33	trente-trois etc.	88	quatre-vingt-huit
4	quatre	40	quarante	89	quatre-vingt-neuf
5	cinq	41	quarante et un(e)	90	quatre-vingt-dix
6	six	42	quarante-deux	91	quatre-vingt-onze
7	sept	43	quarante-trois etc.	92	quatre-vingt-douze
8	huit	50	cinquante	93	quatre-vingt-treize
9	neuf	51	cinquante et un(e)	94	quatre-vingt-quatorze
10	dix	52	cinquante-deux		
11	onze	53	cinquante-trois etc.	95	quatre-vingt-quinze
12	douze	60	soixante	96	quatre-vingt-seize
13	treize	61	soixante et un(e)	97	quatre-vingt-dix-sept
14	quatorze	62	soixante-deux etc.		
15	quinze	70	soixante-dix	98	quatre-vingt-dix-huit
16	seize	71	soixante et onze		
17	dix-sept	72	soixante-douze	99	quatre-vingt-dix-neuf
18	dix-huit	73	soixante-treize		
19	dix-neuf	74	soixante-quatorze	100	cent
20	vingt	75	soixante-quinze	101	cent un(e)
21	vingt et un(e)	76	soixante-seize	110	cent dix
22	vingt-deux	77	soixante-dix-sept	180	cent quatre vingts
23	vingt-trois	78	soixante-dix-huit	200	deux cents
24	vingt-quatre	79	soixante-dix-neuf	201	deux cent un(e)
25	vingt-cinq	80	quatre-vingt(s)	1000	mille
26	vingt-six	81	quatre-vingt-un(e)	2000	deux mille
27	vingt-sept	82	quatre-vingt-deux	1.000.000	un million
28	vingt-huit	83	quatre-vingt-trois	2.000.000	deux millions
29	vingt-neuf	84	quatre-vingt-quatre		

Note:
21, 31, 41, 51, 61 are formed using **et**.
The number **70** is formed from **60** and **10**, while **80** is **4 x 20**, and **90** is **4 x 20 + 10**.
From **100** onwards the hyphen is omitted. **1000** doesn't change.

Years can be expressed in two ways:

2016:	deux mille seize or vingt cent seize

Perfect tense formed with *avoir* (to have)

J'ai téléphoné à Claire deux fois.	I phoned Claire twice.
Elle a aimé le film.	She liked the movie.

The **perfect tense (passé composé)** is formed with the **avoir** and the **past participle** of the main verb. The past participle of regular verbs is simply formed by replacing the infinitive ending *-er* with *é*: e.g. **téléphoné, parlé**.

For some verbs, mostly verbs of movement such as **aller** to go, or reflexive verbs such as **se laver** to wash oneself, **être** is used to form the **passé composé**. For more on this, see Day 7 on page 68.

The passé composé with *avoir*

avoir	past participle	infinitive
j'ai	téléphoné à Claire	telephoner to call
tu as	cherché le plan	chercher to search
il/elle a	aimé le film	aimer to like
nous avons	parlé français	parler to speak
vous avez	nagé 1000 mètres	nager to swim
ils/elles ont	accompagné Claire	accompager to accompany

Exercises

Exercise 1

Fill in the correct number.

trois ....

quatre ....

cinquante ....

seize ....

treize ....

quarante ....

quinze ....

six ....

trente ....

quatorze ....

cinq ....

soixante ....

sept ....

quatre-vingt-huit ....

neuf ....

soixante-dix ....

soixante-dix-huit ....

huit ....

quatre-vingt-dix ....

onze ....

trente et un ....

cent un ....

quatre-vingt-un ....

soixante et onze ....

cent quatorze ....

cinq cents ....

cinquante mille ....

trois mille ....

mille sept cent quatre-vingt-neuf

....

mille neuf cent dix-huit ....

dix-sept cent quatre-vingt-neuf

....

deux millions ....

Exercise 2

Write out in words the years listed in 1 to 8 below and then connect them with the correct historical event!

1 1492 ....

2 1789 ....

3 1912 ....

4 1945 ....

5 1961 ....

6 1980 ....

7 1981 ....

8 1989 ....

a Mort (death) de John Lennon

b François Mitterand président

c la Révolution française

d la Chute du Mur de Berlin (Fall of the Berlin Wall)

e Christophe Colomb découvre (discovers) l'Amérique

f John Kennedy président

g le naufrage (sinking) du Titanic

h Hiroshima

1........ **2**........ **3**........ **4**........ **5**........ **6**........ **7**........ **8**........

Exercise 3

Use avoir to form the perfect tense.

1 Je cherche un plan du métro. ....

2 J'accompagne Claire à la gare. ....

3 Elle parle de ses vacances en Bretagne. ....

4 Elle aime le ski nautique (water ski). ....

5 Elle commence un cours intensif de français. ....

6 Nous téléphonons à Caroline. . ...

Exercice 4

Match the questions below with the correct answers, a, b, c or d.

1 A qui le tour ?

2 Qu'est-ce qu'il vous faut ?

3 Vous désirez autre chose ?

4 Et avec ça ?

a Donnez-moi un kilo de tomates.

b Ça sera tout.

c Une salade.

d C'est à moi.

1 ....   **2** ....   **3** ....   **4** ....

Vocabulary

Below is a list of vocabulary encountered in this chapter.

à plus tard	*later*	**malade**	*sick*
à	*at, to*	**Mamie**	*grandma*
aller voir	*to go to see*	**marchand**	*(vegetable) merchant/*
attendre	*to wait (attends)*	**(de légumes)** *m*	*vendor*
avant	*before*	**mort**	*death*
avoir le temps de	*to have time to*	**marché** *m*	*market*
c'est tout	*that's all*	**naufrage** *m*	*sinking*
ça fait... (faire)	*that's... (to do/make)*	**pas cher**	*not expensive*
ça sera tout	*that'll be all*	**passer à**	*to go (to)*
cet après-midi	*this afternoon*	**pharmacie** *f*	*pharmacy*
déjà	*already*	**pomme** *f*	*apple*
demander	*to ask*	**quartier** *m*	*neighborhood/district*
désirer	*to like*	**s'il vous plaît**	*please*
(désirez)		**s.v.p.** *(abbrv.)*	*please*
en plus	*on top of*	**salade** *f*	*lettuce*
faire les	*to go shopping*	**service** *m*	*favor*
courses		**superbe**	*superb/very nice*
frisée *f*	*frisee lettuce*	**téléphoner à**	*to phone someone*
fruit *m*	*fruit*	**tomate** *f*	*tomato*
il est 11 heures	*it is 11 o'clock*	**trop de**	*too much (of)*
il s'agit de	*it is about/ has to do with*	**Tu pourrais ?**	*Could you?*
(s'agir de)		**(pouvoir)**	*(to be able to/can)*
Je vous en	*How many do you want?*	**venir**	*to come*
mets combien ?		**voilà !**	*here you go!*
kilo *m*	*kilogram/kilogramme*		
laitue *f*	*lettuce*		

day: 5
The family

Day 5 discusses family life and general activities. You will learn the present and past tense of verbs ending in *-ir* and *-re*, and get a brief introduction to the imperative which is used for giving commands. You will also further build your vocabulary and be able to practice what you have learnt.

TRADITIONS...

*In France, everyone (traditionally) has a name day, celebrating the saint's day that they are named after. In some families, name days are even more important than birthdays. Usually, small presents and flowers are given to the person on their name day and many people will wish you **Bonne fête !***

German conversation: Une journée avec les enfants

Claire:	Julie, Annick, qu'est-ce qu'on fait cet après-midi ?
Annick:	On attend Florent, c'est sa fête aujourd'hui, il rentre à 4 heures.
Julie:	Hier, tu as promis de faire des crêpes, c'est une surprise.
Claire:	D'accord, on fait des crêpes pour le goûter et ce soir pas de cuisine !
Annick:	Bonne idée, de toute façon les parents ne sont pas là. Ecoute, encore un quart d'heure pour finir mes devoirs et je peux t'aider. Si tu veux, commence avec Julie.
Claire:	Bon, mais viens quand même me montrer où sont les affaires dans la cuisine.
Annick:	On a besoin de quoi pour faire les crêpes ?
Claire:	D'un grand saladier et d'un mixer.Annick: Alors, prends le grand saladier en plastique rouge qui est dans le placard sous l'évier, en bas. Le mixer est sur l'étagère au dessus du frigo. Si tu préfères travailler la pâte avec une cuillère en bois, c'est dans le tiroir de la table.
Claire:	Je vais me débrouiller.
Annick:	Les parents rentrent tard aujourd'hui, on pourrait tous aller au cinéma à 6 heures.
Julie:	Ouais, super !
Claire:	Pourquoi pas! Le Roi des Lions passe à côté à Odéon, il y a une séance à 6 heures.
Annick:	Bonne idée, Florent adore aller au ciné.
Claire:	Moi aussi.
Julie:	Je sucre les crêpes ?
Claire:	Si tu veux, mais pas trop de sucre comme la dernière fois !

4 heures, des bruits de pas dans l'escalier, Florent arrive.

Annick, Julie, Claire:	Bonne fête, Florent !
Florent:	Salut les filles ! Tiens, ça sent bon. Vous m'avez fait des crêpes pour ma fête ! C'est sympa !
Claire:	Après si tu as envie, on t'invite au ciné, le Roi des Lions passe à Odéon.
Florent:	Génial !

English conversation: A day with the children

Claire:	Julie, Annick, what are we going to do this afternoon?
Annick:	We are waiting for Florent. It's his name day today. He'll be back by 4 o'clock.
Julie:	Yesterday you promised to make crêpes as a surprise for him.
Claire:	OK, let's make crêpes as an afternoon snack and we'll skip dinner tonight.
Annick:	Good idea, our parents aren't going to be there anyway. Listen, I just need another 15 minutes to finish my homework and then I can help you. If you want, you can start already with Julie.
Claire:	All right, but show me where things are kept in the kitchen.
Annick:	What do you need to make crêpes?
Claire:	A large bowl and a mixer.
Annick:	Take the large red plastic bowl that is in the cupboard underneath the sink. The mixer is on the shelf above the fridge. If you prefer to make the dough with a wooden spoon, you'll find that in the table drawer.
Claire:	I'll manage.
Annick:	Our parents are coming back late tonight; we could all go to the movies at 6 o'clock.
Julie:	Yeah, great!
Claire:	Why not? "The Lion King" is on at the Odeon around the corner. There's a showing at 6 o'clock.
Annick:	Good idea! Florent loves going to the movies.
Claire:	Me too.
Julie:	Shall I sprinkle the crêpes with sugar?
Claire:	If you want, but not as much sugar as the last time!

4 p.m., the sound of footsteps coming up the stairs, Florent arrives.

Annick, Julie, Claire:	All the best on your name day, Florent!
Florent:	Hi girls! Now that smells good. You made crêpes on my name day! That's really nice of you!
Claire:	Afterwards, we'd like to invite you to the movies, if you want to go? The Lion King is on at the Odéon.
Florent:	Great!

Grammar

on and nous

Qu'est-ce qu'on fait cet après-midi ?	Qu'est-ce que nous faisons cette après-midi ?
What are we going to do this afternoon?	

In everyday usage the indefinite pronoun on (one) can replace the first person plural nous (we). On is used only as a subject pronoun and always takes a verb in the singular.

Present tense - verbs ending in -ir and -re

To form the present tense of verbs ending in -ir and -re, simply drop the -ir or -re and replace by the endings in the tables below. The verbs finir (to finish) and attendre (to wait) are given as examples.

verbs ending in -ir	ending	finir (to finish)
je/j' ...	-is	je finis
tu ...	-is	tu finis
il/elle ...	-it	il/elle finit
nous	-issons	nous finissons
vous ...	-issez	vous finissiez
ils/elles ...	-issent	ils/elles finissent

verbs ending in -re	ending	attendre (to wait)
je/j' ...	-s	j'attends
tu ...	-s	tu attends
il/elle ...	-	il/elle attend
nous	-ons	nous attendons
vous ...	-ez	vous attendez
ils/elles ...	-ent	ils/elles attendent

also: choisir (to choose), remplir (to fill in), répondre (to answer), vendre (to sell)

Past participle of verbs ending in -ir and -re

ending in -i: fini
j'ai fini, tu as fini *etc.*
ending in -u: attendu
j'ai attendu, tu as attendu *etc.*

The imperative

The imperative is formed from the **second person singular** or the **second person plural of the present tense**.

However, for verbs ending in **-er**, drop the **s** in the second person singular.

Commence déjà avec Julie !	Start already with Julie!
Commencez sans moi !	Start without me!
Remplis le formulaire !	Complete the form!
Choisissez le menu !	Choose the menu!
Attends !	Wait!
Attendez Claire !	Wait for Claire!

Exercises

Exercise 1

Replace nous with on and change the form of the verb accordingly.

1 Nous choisissons un film. ....

2 Nous allons au café. ....

3 Nous téléphonons à Claire. ....

4 Nous attendons Claire. ....

5 Nous prenons le bus. ....

6 Nous rentrons à 8 heures. ....

7 Nous faisons des crêpes. ....

Exercise 2

Fill in the correct form of the verb in brackets using the present tense.

1 Elle (choisir) .... le programme de cinéma.

2 Nous (attendre) .... Florent.

3 Je (remplir) .... le formulaire d'inscription.

4 Vous (attendre) .... Claire ?

5 Je (attendre) .... les parents.

Exercise 3

Rewrite each sentence in the present tense.

1 Nous avons accompagné Claire à l'Alliance française.

....

2 Ils ont fini le test à 6 heures.

....

3 J'ai travaillé cet après-midi.

....

4 On a attendu Claire au café à 7 heures.

....

5 Elle a pris un thé.

....

6 On a invité Claire au cinéma.

....

Exercise 4

What do you say, if you ...

1 ... need something? ....

   a j'ai besoin de ...   **b** je veux ...

2 ... want to congratulate someone on their name day? ....

   a Bonne idée !   **b** Bonne fête !

3 ... want to make a suggestion? ....

   a c'est sympa !   **b** on pourrait aller au cinéma !

Exercise 5

Something in each line is out of place. What is it?

1 le tiroir	le saladier	la cuillère	le mixer
2 le café	le cinéma	la gare	la cuisine
3 aujourd'hui	à 6 heures	la fête	le matin
4 la salade	la surprise	les tomates	les crêpes
5 le petit déjeuner	le déjeuner	le pain	le goûter
6 sur	sous	pour	dans

1................. **2**................. **3**.................

4................. **5**................. **6**.................

Exercise 6

Fill in the correct verb endings.

1 Je m'appell............................ Caroline.

2 Je te présent...........................Patrick.

3 Vous téléphon........................ à Caroline.

4 Elle deman............................ le programme.

5 Le film commenc.................... à 6 heures.

6 Tu accompagn........................ Claire au marché.

7 Vous rentr.............................. tard.

8 Les enfants ador..................... les crêpes.

9 Tu arriv................................... à la gare de l'Est.

10 Ils aim.................................. faire du ski.

Vocabulary

Below is a list of vocabulary encountered in this chapter.

à côté de	*near to/beside*	**goûter** *m*	*snack*
adorer	*to love*	**grand** *m* /**grande** *f*	*large, big*
affaires *f pl*	*things*	**hier**	*yesterday*
aider	*to help*	**idée** *f*	*idea*
attendre	*to wait (for)*	**inviter**	*to invite*
au dessus (de)	*over*	**la dernière fois**	*the last time*
aujourd'hui	*today*	**moi aussi**	*me too*
avoir besoin de	*to need something*	**ou**	*or*
avoir envie (de)	*to want to*	**où**	*where/where to*
bon *adv.*	*well*	**ouais**	*yes, yeah*
bon, bonne *adj.*	*good*	**parents** *m pl*	*parents*
bruit *m*	*noise, sound*	**pas** *m*	*(foot)step*
ça sent …	*that smells…*	**passer**	*to pass, to show (a movie)*
sentir	*to smell*	**placard** *m*	*cupboard*
ce soir	*this evening*	**promis**	*promised*
ciné *m*	*cinema*	**promettre**	*to promise*
comme	*how*	**quand même**	*all the same*
commencer	*to start*	**quart d'heure** *m*	*quarter of an hour/15 min*
crêpe *f*	*crêpe, pancake*	**rentrer**	*to return*
cuillère *f*	*spoon*	**roi** *m*	*king*
cuisine *f*	*kitchen*	**rouge**	*red*
de toute façon	*anyway, in any case*	**saladier** *m*	*bowl*
devoirs *m pl*	*homework*	**se débrouiller**	*to manage*
dire (dis)	*to say*	**séance** *f*	*showing*
écouter	*to listen*	**sous**	*underneath*
en bas	*below, down*	**sucre** *m*	*sugar*
en bois/plastique	*(made) of wood/plastic*	**sucrer**	*to sprinkle with sugar*
escalier *m*	*staircase, stairs*	**surprise** *f*	*surprise*
étagère *f*	*shelf*	**sympa**	*nice*
évier *m*	*sink*	**table** *f*	*table*
faire la cuisine	*to cook*	**tard**	*late*
finir	*to end, to finish*	**tiroir** *m*	*drawer*
cet après-midi	*this afternoon*	**tous**	*all*
génial	*great, super*	**travailler**	*to work*

Test 1

Work your way around the board. Each correct answer will take you to the next question until you have completed the exercise. Enjoy!

1

Choose one of the two answers. Then go to the square with the number of your answer.

2

... cherchons la rue de Fleurus.
Nous ► 8
Vous ► 15

3

Wrong!

Go back to 5.

8

Right! Continue: ... ai faim.
Je ► 6
J' ► 25

9

Wrong!

Go back to 25.

10

Wrong!

Go back to 14.

11

Wrong!

Go back to 29.

16

Good! Continue: ... rentre à midi.
Je ► 22
Ils ► 18

17

Wrong!

Go back to 22.

18

Wrong!

Go back to 16.

19

Correct!

End of exercise

24

Wrong!

Go back to 12.

25

Great! Continue: ... fait les courses.
On ► 14
Tu ► 9

26

Wrong!

Go back to 30.

27

Good! Continue: ... êtes gentil.
Tu ► 23
Vous ► 12

4
Good! Continue:
… font du ski
Ils   ▶ 20
On   ▶ 7

5
Right! Continue:
… prenez le petit
déjeuner.
Nous   ▶ 3
Vous   ▶ 13

6
Wrong!

Go back to 8.

7
Wrong!

Go back to 4.

12
Excellent! Continue: …
sont trois.
Ils   ▶ 16
Nous   ▶ 24

13
Right! Continue:
… commences un cours.
Je   ▶ 21
Tu   ▶ 29

14
Very good! Continue:
… rentrez tard.
Tu   ▶
10 Vous   ▶ 30

15
Wrong!

Go back to 2.

20
Well done! Continue:
… avez des pommes?
Vous   ▶ 5
Tu   ▶ 28

21
Wrong!

Go back to 13.

22
Right! Continue:
… vais au cinéma.
Il   ▶ 17
Je   ▶ 19

23
Wrong!

Go back to 27.

28
Wrong!

Go back to 20.

29
Well done! Continue:
… vont à la piscine.
Ils   ▶ 27
Il   ▶ 11

30
Right! Continue:
… est malade.
Elle   ▶ 4
Elles   ▶ 26

day: 6
Education

Day 6 discusses the French education system. You will learn how to ask more involved questions, how to tell the time and form negative statements. You will further increase your vocabulary and become more at ease understanding and speaking French.

THE SCHOOL SYSTEM...

In France, children start school at the age of six, but the majority will have already gone to an école maternelle *(pre-school) from the age of three. Afterwards, children attend the* école primaire *(primary school) for five years, where they spend the whole day at school. Secondary school extends over a period of five years at a* collège *where they will do their* brevet *examinations. Students wishing to go on to university must obtain their* baccalauréat *and spend another three years in high school, known as a* lycée.

French conversation: Inscription à l'école de langue

Claire:	Bonjour madame, vous m'avez donné un programme des cours il y a une semaine. Aujourd'hui je voudrais m'inscrire pour le test.
Secrétaire:	Oui, vous avez choisi votre niveau ?
Claire:	J'aimerais faire un cours moyen, 4 heures par jour, le matin si possible.
Secrétaire:	Bon, je vous inscris pour le test d'évaluation du niveau correspondant, vous pouvez venir le passer demain matin ?
Claire:	D'accord, à quelle heure?
Secrétaire:	A huit heures et demie, en salle 3 au rez-de-chaussée.
Claire:	Je n'ai pas assez d'argent liquide sur moi pour payer le cours, vous acceptez les chèques ?
Secrétaire:	Pas de problèmes. Vous avez une pièce d'identité ?
Claire:	Voilà mon passeport.
Secrétaire:	Très bien, vous permettez... Merci.
Claire:	Quand est-ce qu'on a les résultats de ce test ?
Secrétaire:	Voyons, niveau moyen 50 candidats, nous affichons les résultats demain soir vers 18 heures dans le hall.
Claire:	Encore une question, est-ce que j'ai le droit de me servir d'un dictionnaire pour le test ?
Secrétaire:	Non, vous n'en avez pas besoin, il y a une partie orale sous forme d'un entretien de dix minutes et une partie écrite avec des exercices à choix multiples.
Claire:	Très bien, merci et à demain.
Secrétaire:	A demain, bonne chance pour le test.

English conversation: Enrolment in the language school

Claire:	Good morning. A week ago you gave me a programme of courses. Today I would like to register for the assessment test.
Secretary:	Yes, have you decided at which level?
Claire:	I want to take an intermediate course, 4 hours a day, if possible in the morning.
Secretary:	Good, then I'll enroll you for the assessment test at that level. Can you take the test tomorrow morning?
Claire:	OK, at what time?
Secretary:	At half past eight in room 3 on the ground floor.
Claire:	I don't have enough cash on me to pay for the course. Do you accept cheques?
Secretary:	No problem. Do you have any form of identification on you?
Claire:	Here's my passport.
Secretary:	Very good, may I? ... Thank you.
Claire:	When will I know the test results?
Secretary:	Let's see, intermediate level, 50 candidates, we will post the results in the entrance hall at about 6 o'clock tomorrow evening.
Claire:	One more question: Am I allowed to use a dictionary for the test?
Secretary:	No, you won't need one. There's an oral part consisting of ten minutes of conversation and a written part with multiple choice questions.
Claire:	Great. Thank you and see you tomorrow.
Secretary:	Goodbye. See you tomorrow. Good luck with the test.

Grammar

Questions with est-ce que

In Day 3 you learnt how to ask questions formed by intonation. Another way to ask questions is by using Est-ce que. Est-ce que is always placed at the beginning of a sentence. By adding est-ce que to a statement, it becomes a question.

Est-ce que j'ai le droit de me servir d'un dictionnaire ?
Am I allowed to use a dictionary?

Negation

The **ne** is often dropped in **spoken language** and **colloquial speech**. For example, instead of **je n'ai pas d'argent** you will often hear **j'ai pas d'argent !** In written Frech, it must always be included.

a) If the **negative** refers to a **verb**, it is divided into two parts, which go before and after the verb. If the verb starts with a vowel or a silent h, **ne** becomes **n'**.

ne ... pas	not
ne ... plus	no more/longer
ne ... jamais	never
ne ... pas de/d'	no
ne ... plus de/d'	no more/longer
ne ... jamais de	never

Examples:

Je *ne* téléphone *pas* à Claire.	I don't phone Claire.
Je *ne* suis *pas* en voiture.	I am not here by car.
Je *ne* suis *plus* à Berlin.	I am no longer in Berlin.
Je *ne* commence *jamais* à 9 heures.	I never start at 9 o'clock.
Je *n'*ai *pas* le programme.	I don't have the programme.

b) If the **negative** refers to a **quantity**, you need to use:
ne ... pas de ..., ne ... plus de ..., ne ... jamais de ...
A verb starting with a **vowel** or a **silent h** takes ne ... pas d'..., ne ... plus d'..., ne ... jamais d'...
The indefinite articles **un**, **une**, **des** and the partitive articles **du**, **de la** are replaced with **de**.

Examples:

Tu as *du* café ? Non, je *n'*ai *pas de* café, j'ai *du* thé.
Do you have coffee? No, I don't have coffee, I have tea.
Tu prends *une* bière ? Non, je *ne* prends *pas de* bière, je *n'*ai *pas* soif.
Are you having a beer? No, I'm not having a beer, I am not thirsty.
Tu as 20 euros ? Non, je *n'*ai *pas* d'argent sur moi.

Have you got 20 euros? No I don't have any money on me.

Vous avez *des* tomates ? Non, *je n'ai plus de* tomates.

Have you got tomatoes? No, I don't have tomatoes any more.

Vous faites *du* ski ? Non, *je ne* fais jamais *de* sport.

Do you go skiing? No, I never do sport.

Time

Time can be expressed in a number of different ways in French.

À quelle heure ?	At what time?
Quelle heure est-il ?	What time is it?
Il est/C'est … 9 heures	It is … 9 o'clock.

In ordinary conversation, time is generally expressed as shown on the left below.

9h	neuf heures	(du matin)
9h05	neuf heures cinq	
9h10	neuf heures dix	
9h15	neuf heures et quart	neuf heures quinze
9h25	neuf heures vingt-cinq	
9h30	neuf heures et demie	neuf heures trente
9h40	dix heures moins vingt	neuf heures quarante
9h45	dix heures moins le quart	neuf heures quarante-cinq
9h50	dix heures moins dix	neuf heures cinquante
9h55	dix heures moins cinq	neuf heures cinquante-cinq
12h	midi	douze heures
14h	deux heures (de l'après-midi)	quatorze heures
22h	dix heures (du soir)	vingt-deux-heures
24h	minuit	zéro heure
9h30'20"	neuf heures trente minutes (et) vingt secondes	

Exercises

Excerise 1

Form questions using **est-ce que** as in the following example.

... (tu/aller faire) les courses? – Oui, d'accord.

Est-ce que tu vas faire les courses ? – Oui, d'accord.

1 ....

(vous / avoir) une pièce d'identité ? – Oui, un passeport.

2 ....

(tu / rentrer) tard ? - Non, vers sept heures du soir.

3 ....

(vous / aimer) faire du ski ? – Oui, du ski de fond.

4 ....

(tu / prendre) le métro ? – Non, le bus.

5 ....

(vous / téléphoner) à Claire ? – Oui, à six heures.

6 ....

(vous / avoir) une voiture ? – Non, une moto (motorbike).

7 ....

(tu / pouvoir) passer à la pharmacie ? – Oui, après le cours.

8 ....

(vous / prendre) du café au petit déjeuner ? – Non, du thé.

Exercise 2

Follow the example below and answer using a negative form.

Vous aimez le jazz ? (ne … pas / le rock)   **Non, je n'aime pas le jazz, j'aime le rock.**

1 Vous prenez le bus ? (ne … pas / le métro)

Non, ...

2 Tu travailles à York ? (ne … pas / à Londres)

Non, ...

3 Vous avez soif ? (ne … pas / avoir faim)

Non, ...

4 Vous rentrez à 5 heures ? (ne… pas / à 7 heures)

Non, ...

5 Tu commences à 9 heures ? (ne … pas / à 8 heures et demie)

Non, ...

6 Vous attendez Annick ? (ne … pas / Florent)

Non, ...

Exercise 3

What shopping have we left to do? Form sentences as in the following example.

On a encore (still) du café ?   **Non, on … (ne … plus de) Non, on n'a plus de café.**

1 On a encore des fruits ? Non, on … (ne … plus de)

....

2 On a encore du sucre ? Non, on … (ne … plus de

....

3 On a encore du chocolat ? Non, on … (ne … plus de)

....

4 On a encore de la confiture ? Non, on … (ne plus … de)

....

5 On a encore du pain ? Non, on … (ne … plus de)

....

Exercise 4

Connnect the questions with the right answers.

1 Tu prends le bus ?		**a** Non, je ne fais pas de ski.
2 Tu fais du ski ?		**b** Non, je n'ai plus de plan.
3 Tu as un plan de Paris ?		**c** Non, je n'ai pas de bagages.
4 Tu as un dictionnaire ?		**d** Non, je n'ai pas besoin de visa.
5 Tu as besoin d'un visa ?		**e** Non, je ne prends jamais le bus.
6 Tu as des bagages ?		**f** Non, je n'ai pas de dictionnaire.

1........ **2**........ **3**........ **4**........ **5**........ **6**........

Exercise 5

Claire has written down her fixed daily schedule. Write out the times in French and put the verbs in brackets in the correct form.

8.30 **A *huit heures et demie*, le cours** (commencer) ***commence.***

1 10.45.. ,
on (prendre) .... un café à la cafétéria.

2 12.15 .... ,
je (aller) .... déjeuner avec Caroline.

3 14.30 .... ,
je (passer) .... à la banque.

4 15.10 .... ,
je (prendre) .... le métro.

5 15.25 .... ,
je (arriver) ....à place de l'Odéon.

6 15.30 .... ,
je (rencontrer) .... Florent.

7 17.45 .... ,
on (aller) .... au cinéma.

Vocabulary

Below is a list of vocabulary encountered in this chapter.

à huit heures et demie	*at half past eight*	**j'aimerais (aimer)**	*I would like (to like)*
A quelle heure ?	*At what time?*	**le matin**	*morning*
accepter	*to take, to accept*	**liquide**	*cash (money); liquid*
afficher	*to display*	**niveau** *m*	*level*
argent *m*	*money*	**oral**	*oral*
assez (de)	*enough (of)*	**par jour**	*daily*
avoir besoin de	*to need something*	**partie** *f*	*part*
avoir le droit	*to be allowed to*	**pas de problème**	*no problem*
Bonne chance !	*Good luck!*	**passeport** *m*	*passport*
chance *f*	*luck*	**passer un test**	*to take a test*
chèque *m*	*cheque*	**payer**	*to pay*
correspondant	*accordingly*	**permettre**	*to allow, permit, let*
cours moyen *m*	*intermediate level*	**pièce d'identité** *f*	*ID*
demain matin	*tomorrow morning*	**problème** *m*	*problem*
demain soir	*tomorrow evening*	**programme des cours** *m*	*program(me) of courses*
dictionnaire *m*	*dictionary*		
donner	*to give*	**question** *f*	*question*
écrit	*written*	**résultat** *m*	*result*
entretien *m*	*conversation*	**rez-de-chaussée** *m*	*ground floor*
évaluation *f*	*assessment*	**salle** *f*	*room*
exercice *m* **à choix multiple**	*multiple choice exercise*	**se servir de**	*to use*
		semaine *f*	*week*
inscription *f*	*enrol(l)ment*	**si possible**	*if possible*
hall *m*	*entrance hall*	**sous forme de**	*in the form of*
il y a (une semaine)	*(one week) ago*	**sur moi**	*with/on me*
		vers	*at about*
inscrire	*to enrol(l)*		

Making friends

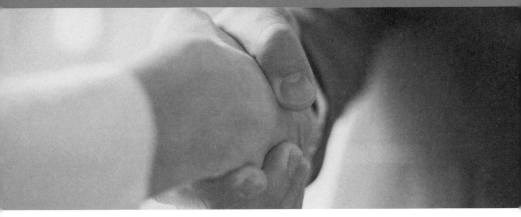

Day 7 is all about making friends. You will learn the names of countries and nationalities and how to make adjectives agree with the noun (masculine and feminine). You will also learn the perfect tense using *être* and how to conjugate the verbs *connaître* (to know) and *venir* (to come).

ETIQUETTE…

*Wherever two people meet, they begin with a formal greeting. To fail to greet someone, even a supermarket check-out assistant, is considered rude. The average French person is capable of kissing or shaking hands with a whole room of people before starting a conversation or getting down to business. The number of kisses given varies between two and four, depending on the region. It is also worth remembering that everyone scrupulously respects the distinction between **vous** (polite) and **tu** (informal).*

French conversation: Premiers contacts

A la cafétéria, après le premier cours à l'Alliance française, Claire, Luis, un étudiant argentin, et Miko, une étudiante japonaise.

Luis:	J'ai trouvé le prof très sympa et vous ?
Claire:	Moi aussi, mais je ne suis pas tout à fait au niveau, j'ai des problèmes de grammaire.
Miko:	C'est normal. On pourrait se présenter, moi c'est Miko. Je suis japonaise. Je suis arrivée à Paris il y a six mois, et vous ?
Luis:	Moi je viens de Buenos Aires, j'ai une formation d'informaticien, j'ai 30 ans, je travaille pour une entreprise française en Argentine.
Claire:	Je m'appelle Claire, je suis anglaise. Je suis secrétaire bilingue. J'habite dans une famille dans le sixième.
Luis:	Vous connaissez d'autres pays en Europe, Miko ?
Miko:	Je suis restée un an en Angleterre à Londres avant de venir ici.
Luis:	Qu'est-ce que vous faites dans la vie ?
Miko:	Je ne travaille pas encore. J'ai une bourse pour un an à Paris. Je fais des études de musique au Conservatoire.
Claire:	Vous parlez très bien français! C'est votre premier séjour en France ?
Miko:	Oui, mais au Japon j'ai eu un copain français. Si vous voulez, on pourrait se tutoyer !
Luis:	D'accord ! Vous, pardon, tu viens demain à la visite guidée de Versailles ?
Miko:	Non, je préfère aller visiter le Marais.
Claire:	Je peux t'accompagner ?
Miko:	Avec plaisir. On se retrouve place de l'Hôtel de ville à 2 heures ? Luis, si tu veux, tu peux nous rejoindre à »la Tartine« rue de Rivoli vers 6 h ?
Luis:	Entendu.
Claire:	Alors à demain après-midi.

English conversation: First contacts

At the cafeteria, after the first lesson at the Alliance française; Claire; Luis, an Argentinian student; and Miko, a Japanese student.

Luis:	I found the teacher quite nice, didn't you?
Claire:	Me too, but I'm not at that level yet and I have problems with grammar.
Miko:	That's normal. Let me introduce myself: I am Miko. I'm Japanese. I've been in Paris for six months, what about you?
Luis:	I'm from Buenos Aires; I'm training to be an IT specialist; I'm 30 years old and I work for a French company in Argentina.
Claire:	My name is Claire, I am English and a bilingual secretary. I'm staying with a family in the sixth (arrondissement).
Luis:	Have you got to any other countries in Europe, Miko?
Miko:	Before I came here I spent a year in England, *in London*.
Luis:	And what do you do for a living?
Miko:	I am not working yet. I have a scholarship for one year in Paris. I'm studying at the music academy.
Claire:	Your French is very good! Is this your first stay in France?
Miko:	Yes, but I had a French friend back in Japan. If you want you can say 'tu' (informal version of you) to me!
Luis:	OK. Are you going on the guided tour of Versailles tomorrow?
Miko:	No, I prefer to see the Marais quarter.
Claire:	Can I come with you?
Miko:	Certainly. Can we meet at the place de l'Hôtel de ville at 2 o'clock? Luis, if you want to you can join us at around 6 o'clock in the café "la Tartine" in the rue de Rivoli.
Luis:	All right.
Claire.	Well, see you tomorrow afternoon then.

Grammar

Adjectives

Adjectives must agree in gender and in number with the noun to which they refer.

singular/masculine

un étudiant japonais	a (male) Japanese student
il est japonais	he is Japanese

singular/feminine

une étudiante japonaise	a (female) Japanese student
elle est japonaise	she is Japanese

plural/masculine

des étudiants japonais	(male) Japanese students
ils sont japonais	they are Japanese

plural/feminine

des étudiantes japonaises	(female) Japanese students
elles sont japonaises	they are Japanese

If a group includes both males and females the adjective will always take the masculine form.
The difference between the masculine (japonais) and the feminine (japonaise) adjective is audible when the final consonant (here s) is voiced before an e. A number of adjectives don't have a feminine form, because they already end in an -e, e.g. moderne, sympathique: il est sympathique/elle est sympathique. Short forms like sympa (sympathique), super (superb) don't change.

Countries and nationalities

Countries are either feminine or masculine. If they start with a vowel the definite articles le and la change to l'. When specifying a location, e.g. in France, you use en for feminine country names and for masculine country names starting with a vowel - en France.
For masculine country names starting with a consonant and for country names in the plural, you need to use au or aux - au Japon, au Portugal, aux États-Unis
For cities you always use à - elle habite à Paris, à Tokyo.

venir de to come from, to originate from	venir à to come to

l'Europe *f*	Europe
un pays européen	
une institution européenne	
l'Union européenne (EU) *f*	
la France	France
Michel est français	
Caroline est française	
un séjour en France	
l'Angleterre *f*	England
John est anglais	
Mary est anglaise	
un séjour en Angleterre/il est en Angleterre	
l'Allemagne *f*	Germany
Karl est allemand	
Helga est allemande	
l'Espagne *f*	Spain
José est espagnol	
Carmen est espagnole	
l'Italie *f*	Italy
Giovanni est italien	
Carla est italienne	
la Suède	Sweden
Sven est suédois	
Kirstin est suédoise	
l'Argentine *f*	Argentina
Luis est argentin	
Maria est argentine	
Un séjour en Argentine	
le Japon	Japan
Yoschi est japonais	
Miko est japonaise	
Un séjour au Japon	
le Portugal	Portugal
Un séjour au Portugal	
Joaquin est portugais	
Dolorès est portugaise	
les États-Unis	United States of America
Un séjour aux États-Unis.	
Joe est américain	
Emily est américaine	

Perfect tense with *être*

Some verbs form the perfect tense (**passé composé**) using **être**, e.g. **arriver** (to arrive), **rester** (to stay), **aller** (to go), **venir** (to come), **rentrer** (to return, to come home).

Examples:

je suis arrivé(e) à Paris
tu es arrivé(e) à Londres
il est arrivé à Lyon
elle est arrivée à Grenoble
vous êtes arrivé(e) à Madrid
nous sommes arrivé(e)s à York
vous êtes arrivé(e)s à Cannes
ils sont arrivés à Buenos Aires
elles sont arrivées à Nice (Nizza)

Note:

For verbs whose perfect tense is formed with **être**, the **participle** (**arrivé**) agrees with the number and gender of the subject of the sentence it relates to, e.g. **il est arrivé** but **elles sont arrivées.**

Verbs

connaître (to know)	venir (to come)
present tense:	
je connais	**je viens**
tu connais	**tu viens**
il/elle/on connaît	**il / elle / on vient**
nous connaissons	**nous venons**
vous connaissez	**vous venez**
ils/elles connaissent	**ils/elles viennent**
perfect tense:	
j'ai connu	**je suis venu(e)**

Exercises

Exercise 1

Introduce these people as in the example below.

Miko Yahuto est japonaise, elle vient de Tokyo, elle habite au Japon.

1 Peter Henle/Allemagne/Nuremberg

....

2 Bernadette Martial/France/Lyon

....

3 John et Mary Williams/Angleterre/Londres

....

4 Lucia Cocci/Italie/Florence

....

5 José Fernandez/Espagne/Madrid

....

6 Maria Muricy/Portugal/Lisbonne

....

7 Sven Johansen/Suède/Stockholm

....

Exercise 2

Qu'est-ce qu'ils parlent? What language do they speak?

1 Miko (Japan) parle ....

2 John et Mary (England) parlent ....

3 Nadine (France) parle ....

4 Peter (Germany) parle ....

5 José (Spain) parle ....

6 Carla (Italy) parle ....

7 Sven (Sweden) parle ....

8 Maria (Portugal) parle ....

Exercise 3

Form a sentence by linking up one section from each of the three columns.

Miko	est	rentré à 8 heures
Peter		venus à Versailles
Maria et Carla	sont	restée un an à Paris
John et Sven		arrivées à Nice
Bernadette et José		allés à Londres

1 ....

2 ....

3 ....

4 ....

5 ....

Exercise 4

Form the present tense.

1 Nous sommes venus de York. ....

2 Nous sommes arrivés gare de l'Est. ....

3 Nous avons téléphoné à Claire. ....

4 Nous avons cherché un hôtel. ....

5 Nous sommes restés trois jours (Tage) à Paris. ....

6 Nous avons visité le Marais. ....

7 Nous avons déjeuné dans le quartier. ....

Exercise 5

One word in each line is out of place. Which one?

français	allemand	anglais	moderne	....
Londres	Stockholm	Luis	York	....
bourse	étudiant	argent	études	....
Espagne	Italie	Tokyo	France	....

Vocabulary

Below is a list of vocabulary encountered in this chapter.

arrondissement	*arrondisement (district)*	**la France**	*France*
au Japon	*in Japan*	**le Japon**	*Japan*
autre	*other*	**le Marais**	*a Parisian quarter*
avant de	*before*	**le sixième (6e)**	*the sixth arrondisement*
avoir … ans	*to be … years old*	**arrondisement**	*(in Paris)*
bilingue	*bilingual*	**Londres**	*London*
bourse *f*	*scholarship*	**mois** *m*	*month*
cafétéria *f*	*cafeteria*	**musique** *f*	*music*
connaître	*to know*	**niveau** *m*	*level*
conservatoire *m*	*(music) academy*	**normal**	*normal*
copain *m*	*friend (male)*	**on pourrait**	*we could (pouvoir)*
copine *f*	*friend (female)*	**pas encore**	*not yet*
contact *m*	*contact*	**pays** *m*	*country*
dans	*in*	**problème** *m*	*problem*
demain	*tomorrow afternoon*	**prof m**	*teacher (colloquial)*
après-midi		**professeur** *m*	*teacher*
en France	*in France*	**rejoindre**	*to join*
entendu	*(here) all right*	**rester**	*to stay*
entreprise *f*	*company, business*	**se présenter**	*to introduce oneself*
être au niveau	*to be at that level*	**se retrouver**	*to meet*
étudiant(e) *m(f)*	*student*	**se tutoyer**	*to address each other with*
eu (avoir)	*have had*		*the informal 'tu'*
faire des études	*to study*	**secrétaire** *f*	*secretary*
formation *f*	*training*	**travailler**	*to work*
français(e)	*French, from France*	**très bien**	*very good*
grammaire *f*	*grammar*	**trouver**	*to find*
habiter	*to live, stay*	**venir**	*to come*
ici	*here*	**vers**	*towards*
il y a	*before (temporal)*	**vie** *f*	*life*
informaticien *m*	*IT specialist*	**visite guidée** *f*	*guided tour*
japonais(e)	*Japanese, from Japan*	**visiter**	*to visit*
l'Angleterre *f*	*England*		
l'Argentine *f*	*Argentina*		

day: 8

Sightseeing

Day 8 helps you to build your conversation and comprehension skills and is all about prepositions (to, in, on, etc.) which will help with everything from understanding directions to talking about where you live. You will also further build your vocabulary.

LE MÉTRO

*The **Paris métro** system is a quick and efficient means of getting around the city. Lines are identified by color, number and the name of their terminals so it is easy to use. It runs from 5:30a.m. until 12:30a.m. **Tickets** are valid on both **le métro** and **le bus** but it is much cheaper to buy weekly or monthy cards, or a **carnet** (book) of ten tickets than individual tickets for every journey. Tickets must be validated before going underground.*

French conversation: A la découverte de Paris

Place de l'Hôtel de ville.

Claire:	Salut ! Ça va ? Tu m'attends depuis longtemps ?
Miko:	Non, je viens d'arriver ! Il fait un temps splendide ! On pourrait aller à pied à la place des Vosges, c'est la plus ancienne place de Paris.

Un quart d'heure plus tard.

Miko:	Je ne sais plus où on est. Je crois qu'on s'est trompé ... Pardon, Madame, la place des Vosges, c'est bien dans cette direction ?
Passante:	Ah non, pas du tout ! Par là vous allez au Louvre. La place des Vosges, c'est dans la direction opposée.
Miko:	Comment on y va ?
Passante:	Ce n'est pas difficile. Faites demi-tour et continuez la rue de Rivoli tout droit jusqu'à l'église Saint-Paul et puis tournez à gauche, c'est indiqué.
Miko:	C'est loin d'ici ?
Passante:	Non, à pied, c'est à 20 minutes environ.

Place des Vosges. Il est trois heures.

Claire:	Ouf ! je suis fatiguée. Quelle chaleur !
Miko:	Je n'ai plus envie de marcher. Je crois que le Musée Picasso n'est pas très loin d'ici.
Claire:	J'ai lu dans »Pariscope« que tous les musées sont fermés le mardi.
Miko:	C'est vrai ! J'ai complètement oublié! Qu'est-ce qu'on fait alors ?
Claire:	On marche jusqu'à la place de la Bastille pour voir le nouvel opéra. C'est un chef-d'œuvre d'architecture moderne.
Miko:	D'accord, mais alors on prend le métro pour revenir rue de Rivoli, on a rendez-vous à six heures avec Luis à »la Tartine«.
Claire:	On peut prendre le métro à la place de la Bastille et descendre à Saint-Paul, ça fait une station.

English conversation: Discovering Paris

Place de l'Hôtel de ville.

Claire:	Hello! How are you? Have you been waiting for me for long?
Miko:	No, I just arrived. The weather is fantastic! We could walk to the place des Vosges, it's the oldest square in Paris.

15 minutes later.

Miko:	I don't know where we are any more. I think we're lost. Excuse me, is the place des Vosges in this direction?
Passer-by:	Oh no, not at all! This takes you to the Louvre. The place des Vosges is the opposite direction.
Miko:	How do we get there?
Passer-by:	That's not difficult. Just turn around and continue on the rue de Rivoli until the church of Saint-Paul, then turn left, there is a sign there.
Miko:	Is it far from here?
Passer-by:	No, it is about a 20 minute walk.

Place des Vosges. It is three o'clock.

Claire:	Phew! I am tired. It's hot!
Miko:	I don't want to walk anymore. I think the Picasso Museum isn't that far from here.
Claire:	I read in *Pariscope* that all museums are closed on Tuesdays.
Miko:	That's right! I totally forgot! What are we going to do then?
Claire:	We'll walk up to the place de la Bastille to see the new opera house. It's a masterpiece of modern architecture.
Miko:	OK, but then we'll take the subway to go back to rue de Rivoli. We've got a date with Luis at 6 o'clock in "la Tartine".
Claire:	We can take the subway at place de la Bastille and get off at Saint-Paul, it's one stop.

Grammar

à and *en*

For feminine names of countries (see Day 7) and masculine names of countries beginning with a vowel, the preposition **en** is used. For masculine names of countries starting with a consonant **au** is used.
For plural country names, use **aux**; always use **à** for cities.

| Where? | Claire est *en France*. | Claire est *au Portugal*. |
| Where to? | Karl va *en Allemagne*. | Karl va *au Portugal*. Karl va *à Lyon*. |

In all other cases a verb and **à** + (**article** + **noun**) designates the location (where?) and the direction (where to?); **à** and **le** are joined to form **au**, **à** and **les** to form aux while **à l'** is used before a singular noun beginning with a silent h or a vowel.

aller *à* Paris
aller *au* cinéma/*au* café
téléphoner *au* musée
aller *à l'*hôtel
aller *à la* gare
arriver *à la* gare
prendre le métro *à la* station Saint-Paul

The preposition de

De specifies a starting point or the origin:
Elle vient de Tokyo.   She is coming from Tokyo (right now). She is from Tokyo.

When **de** + **le** are positioned in front of a noun they become **du**, while **de** + **les** become **des**. Before a singular noun beginning with a vowel or a silent h, **de** + **le** and **de** + **la** become **de l'**.

Elle revient du marché.	She returns from the market.
Il vient de la Place des Vosges.	He is coming from the place des Vosges.
J'arrive de l'aéroport.	I'm coming from the airport.
Il revient des États-Unis.	He is coming back from the U.S.A.
Miko parle du Japon.	Miko is talking about Japan.

Other prepositions to describe locations		
à côté de	à côté de Paris	in the vicinity of
	à côté du café	next to/near
	à côté de l'hôtel	
	à côté de la gare	
à gauche		(to the) left
à gauche de	à gauche de Florent	left of/to the left
	à gauche du restaurant	
	à gauche de l'hôtel	
	à gauche de la gare	
	à gauche des	
à droite		(to the) right
à droite de	à droite de Claire	right of/to the right
	à droite du café	
	à droite de l'opéra	
	à droite de la poste	
	à droite des ...	
jusqu'à	jusqu'à Paris	to, as far as, up to,
	jusqu'au musée	until
	jusqu'à l'hôtel	
	jusqu'à la place	
	jusqu'aux...	
loin de	loin de York	far (away) from
	loin du métro	
	loin d'ici	
	loin de la gare	
	loin des ...	
près de	près de Paris	near/nearby
	près du cinéma	in the vicinity of
	près de l'école	
	près de la gare	
	près des ...	
avant	avant Paris	in front of, before
	avant le café	
	avant la pharmacie	
	avant l'hôtel	
	avant les ...	
devant	devant Claire	in front of, outside
	devant le cinéma	
	devant la poste	
	devant l'hôtel	
	devant les ...	

dans	dans le sac	in
	dans la voiture	
	dans les rues	
sur	sur le pont (bridge)	on
	sur la table (table)	
	sur l'étagère (shelf)	
	sur les ...	
sous	sous le journal	under/underneath
	sous la table	
	sous l'étagère	
	sous les ...	

Exercises

Exercise 1

Complete the sentences using à, à la or en.

1 José est .... Madrid.

2 Peter habite............................ Allemagne.

3 Nous prenons le métro .... station Bastille.

4 J'attends John .... gare.

5 On marche jusqu' .... la place des Vosges.

6 Lucia va .... Italie.

Exercise 2

Complete the sentences using au, à l' or aux.

1 Je téléphone .... hôtel.

2 Nous sommes .... café.

3 Comment on va .... Louvre ?

4 John habite .... États-Unis.

5 Ils vont .... opéra.

6 Elles arrivent .... musée.

Exercise 3

Complete the sentences using the appropriate word.

Espagne/hôtel/place/Lisbonne/ musée/États-Unis

1 Cet après-midi on va au ....

2 Luis est resté un an aux ....

3 Ils sont arrivés hier en.......................................

4 Marchez jusqu'à la..

5 Elle téléphone à l' ....

Exercice 4

Fill in **du, de la, de l'** or **des** as in the example below.

Elle vient du cinéma? Non, . . . poste.

Non, de la poste.

1 Elle arrive de la gare ? Non, ... aéroport.

2 Ils viennent du restaurant ? Non, ... marché.

3 John vient d'Angleterre ? Non, ... États-Unis.

4 Miko parle du Japon ? Non, ... France.

Exercice 5

Form sentences by linking one name from each column.

La Tour Eiffel   Paris   France

La Tour Eiffel est à Paris en France.

1 La Statue de la Liberté	Munich	Angleterre
2 Big Ben	Madrid	États-Unis
3 Le Prado	Rome	Italie
4 La Fête de la Bière	Londres	Allemagne (Octoberfest)
5 Le Vatican	New-York	Espagne

1 ....

2 ....

3 ....

4 ....

5 ....

Exercise 6

Choose the option that correctly answers the question or completes the sentence.

1 Où est le musée Picasso ?
  a A côté de la place des Vosges.
  b Sous la place des Vosges.

2 Où est Versailles ?
  a loin de Paris
  b près de Paris

3 Continuez ... (until)
  a jusqu'à l'église Saint-Paul
  b avant l'église Saint-Paul

4 Claire attend Miko (in front of)
  a devant la station de métro
  b avant la station de métro

5 Continuez ... (straight ahead)
  a à droite !
  b tout droit !

1 .... 2 .... 3 .... 4 .... 5 ....

Vocabulary

Below is a list of vocabulary encountered in this chapter.

à droite	to the right	**lu (lire)**	read
à gauche	to the left	**marcher**	to walk
à pied	on foot	**métro** m	underground/subway
architecture f	architecture	**moderne**	modern
avoir envie de	to want to (do sth)	**musée** m	museum
avoir rendez-vous	to have an appointment	**nouvel**	new
c'est à 20 minutes	it's about 20 minutes away	**opéra** m	opera house
		opposé	opposite
chaleur f	heat	**Où ?**	Where?
chef-d'œuvre m	masterpiece	**Uuf !**	Phew!
comment	how	**par là**	in this direction
continuer	to continue	**pardon**	excuse me
croire (crois)	to believe	**pas du tout**	not at all
depuis	since	**place** f	square
descendre	to exit	**plus tard**	later
difficile	difficult	**quart d'heure** m	quarter of an hour
direction f	direction	**Quelle chaleur !**	It's so hot!
environ	approximately, about	**revenir**	to return, go back
être dans la direction de	to be in the direction of	**savoir**	to know
		se tromper	to be mistaken
faire demi-tour	to turn around	**splendide**	wonderful/ splendid
fatigué	tired	**station** f	train station
découverte f	discovery	**tourner**	to turn round
il fait un temps…	the weather is …	**tout droit**	straight ahead
jusqu'à	up to, until	**venir de faire**	to have just done
loin de	far from	**qqch**	something
longtemps	long (time), ages		

day: 9

Café culture

Day 9 teaches you how to ask for items in different quantities and how to express your preferences. You will learn how to say that you have to do something using *il faut*, pick up more cultural information about life in France, as well as further build your vocabulary.

THE BILL...

*Waiters should be addressed using **Monsieur** or **Madame**. If the bill says **service compris** (includes service charge), you do not need to leave a tip, although many people leave a few cent change on the plate before leaving.*

French conversation: Rendez-vous au café

Six heures du soir. A »la Tartine«, rue de Rivoli.

Luis:	Salut ! Alors racontez-moi votre balade dans le Marais !
Claire:	Tu sais, on a marché tout l'après-midi, on n'a pas eu de chance. Le musée Picasso était fermé. On a vu beaucoup de vieux cafés. Miko a fait beaucoup de photos.
Garçon:	Messieurs Dames, bonjour. Qu'est-ce que je vous sers ?
Claire:	Je voudrais un café et une eau minérale, s'il vous plaît.
Garçon:	Vittel? Perrier? Vichy ?
Claire:	Un Perrier citron, s'il vous plaît.
Garçon:	Bon, et pour vous mademoiselle ?
Miko:	Pour moi un grand crème, s'il vous plaît.
Garçon:	Et pour Monsieur ?
Luis:	J'ai faim. Qu'est-ce que vous avez comme sandwichs ?
Garçon:	Saucisson-beurre, pâté, gruyère.
Luis:	Je n'aime pas le beurre. Je préfère prendre un sandwich au pâté. Vous avez un grand choix de vins. Qu'est-ce que c'est le Bourgueil ?
Garçon:	C'est un vin rouge des pays de la Loire, excellent et très connu.
Luis:	Alors un verre de Bourgueil. Vous ne voulez rien manger ?
Claire:	Non merci, rien pour moi. Et toi Miko, tu veux quelque chose ?
Miko:	Je n'aime pas les sandwichs, vous avez autre chose ?
Garçon:	Oui, croque-monsieur, salade composée, quiche.
Miko:	Un croque-monsieur, s'il vous plaît. Alors Versailles, ça t'a plu ?
Luis:	C'est immense, un peu trop de touristes. La prochaine fois je fais comme vous, pas de guide ! J'aimerais bien aller au nouveau Louvre.
Miko:	Si on ne veut pas faire la queue trop longtemps, il faut aller au Louvre le matin de bonne heure !
Luis:	Difficile en semaine à cause des cours. Excusez-moi, je dois rentrer chez moi, j'attends un appel d'Argentine. Monsieur! L'addition, s'il vous plaît !

English conversation: Meeting in the café

Six o'clock in the evening; in the café La Tartine on rue de Rivoli.

Luis:	Hello! Tell me about your stroll through the Marais quarter.
Claire:	You know, we spent the entire afternoon walking, but had no luck. The Picasso Museum was closed. We saw a lot of old cafés. Miko took lots of pictures.
Waiter:	Good afternoon! What can I get you?
Claire:	I'd like an espresso and a mineral water, please.
Waiter:	Vittel? Perrier? Vichy?
Claire:	Perrier with a slice of lemon, please.
Waiter:	OK, and for you, miss?
Miko:	For me a large coffee with milk, please.
Waiter:	And for you, sir?
Luis:	I am hungry. What kind of sandwiches do you have?
Waiter:	Salami and butter, pâté, gruyère cheese.
Luis:	I don't like butter. I'd rather have a sandwich with pâté. You have a big selection of wine. What kind of wine is this Bourgueil?
Waiter:	That's an excellent and very famous red wine from the Loire region.
Luis:	A glass of Bourgueil then. Don't you want to eat anything?
Claire:	No thanks, nothing for me. What about you Miko, do you want anything?
Miko:	I don't like sandwiches, do you have anything else?
Waiter:	Yes, croque-monsieur, mixed salad, quiche.
Miko:	The croque-monsieur, please. So, did you enjoy Versailles?
Luis:	It's huge and just a few too many tourists. Next time I'll follow your example, no guide! I'd like to visit the new Louvre.
Miko:	If you don't want to spend half the day waiting in line you'll have to go to the Louvre early!
Luis:	That'll be difficult during the week because of my classes. I'm sorry, I have to go home, I'm waiting for a phone call from Argentina. The bill, please!

Grammar

Quantities

Specifications of quantities are always followed by **de + noun** (without the article **le, la, les**). Nouns starting with a vowel or a silent h take a **d'**.

Nouns specifying quantities: **un kilo de tomates** (one kilogram of tomatoes), **une livre d'abricots** (one pound of apricots), **un verre d'eau** (a glass of water), **une bouteille de vin** (a bottle of wine), **un paquet de cigarettes** (a pack of cigarettes), **une boîte de thon** (a can of tuna).

Adverbs

You can also further specify quantities using adverbs such as: **peu de** (little), **beaucoup de** (plenty of), **assez de** (enough) **trop de** (too much).

J'ai mangé une tablette de chocolat.	I've eaten a bar of chocolate.
Elle a 30 jours de vacances.	She has 30 days holiday (vacation).
Je bois un litre d'eau par jour.	I drink a litre of water per day.
Miko a fait beaucoup de photos.	Miko has taken lots of pictures.
Il mange peu de beurre.	He eats little butter.
J'ai assez de pain.	I have enough bread.
Elle a beaucoup de copains.	She has many friends.
Il y a trop de touristes.	There are too many tourists.
Je *n'*ai pas de chance.	I have no luck.

Expressing preferences

The verbs **aimer, adorer, préférer, détester** are all followed by the definite article **le/la/les**.

J'aime	le champagne	I like
J'adore	la musique classique	I really like
	l'architecture baroque	
Moi, je préfère	le jazz	I like best/I prefer
	l'architecture moderne	
	les films de Godard	
Je n'aime pas	la bière	I don't like
Je n'aime pas du tout	les visites guidées	I cannot stand
Je déteste	les cigarettes	I hate

il faut + infinitive (to have to /to be necessary)

Il faut (falloir in the infinitive) is used with a verb in the infinitive with no preposition.

Il faut payer en liquide.	One has to pay in cash.
Il faut faire la queue.	One must stand in line.

Préférer (to prefer)

present tense:

je préfère	nous préférons
tu préfères	vous préférez
il/elle préfère	ils/elles préfèrent

perfect tense:

j'ai préféré

Exercises

Exercise 1

Follow the example below and connect the appropriate items from the two columns for your shopping list.

	2 kilos	carottes	deux kilos de carottes
1	1 boîte	tomates	....
2	2 bouteilles	chocolat	....
3	1 livre	eau minérale	....
4	3 tablettes	ait (milk)	....
5	1 litre	thon (tuna)	....

Exercise 2

Say what Miko likes or hates.

le   la   l'   les

Miko aime/déteste . . .

1 .... thé

2 .... architecture

3 .... café au lait

4 .... films comiques

5 .... bière

6 .... vin rouge

7 .... musées

Exercise 3

Complete the sentences using the correct form of the present tense of **préférer**:

J'aime beaucoup la musique classique mais je .... le jazz. Tu veux une quiche ou

tu .... un sandwich au gruyère ? Claire aime beau-coup la bière mais elle ....

le vin. Nous aimons beaucoup la télévision mais nous .... le cinéma. Qu'est-ce que

vous .... au petit déjeuner, le café au lait ou le thé ? Ils aiment la littérature classique

mais ils .... la littérature moderne.

Exercise 4

Match the right answers to the corresponding questions.

1 Qu'est-ce que tu prends ?

2 Qu'est-ce que vous avez fait ?

3 Tu connais le Louvre ?

4 On partage ?

5 Versailles, ça t'a plu ?

6 Tu aimes la bière ?

7 Tu as fait la queue ?

8 Qu'est-ce que tu préfères à Paris ?

a Les musées.

b Oui, pendant deux heures !

c Un Perrier citron.

d J'ai pris beaucoup de photos dans le Marais.

e Non, pas encore.

f Non, trop de touristes.

g Non, je vous invite.

h Je préfère le vin.

1........   2........   3........   4........   5........   6........   7........   8........

Exercise 5

Replace devoir with il faut as in the following example.

Nous devons prendre le métro.   *Il faut prendre le métro.*

1 Nous devons faire les courses.

....

2 Nous devons rentrer à sept heures.

....

3 Nous devons rester un an à Paris.

....

4 Nous devons descendre à Odéon.

....

5 Nous devons téléphoner à l'hôtel.

....

6 Nous devons faire la queue devant le musée.

....

7 Nous devons attendre Claire.

....

8 Nous devons commencer à huit heures.

....

Exercise 6

Fill in the quantity in French.

1 Claire a (few) .... copains à Paris.

2 Miko a fait (many) .... photos dans le quartier.

3 Luis a mangé (too many) .... sandwichs.

4 Je bois (two litres) .... eau par jour.

5 Il y a (too many) .... touristes à Versailles.

6 J'ai (few) .... bagages.

7 Tu as (enough) .... argent ?

8 Il mange (little) .... beurre.

Exercise 7

One word in each line does not fit. Which one?

le café	l'addition	le client	le quartier	....
la quiche	la salade	le guide	le croque-monsieur	....
la touriste	le cours	la visite	le musée	....
le sandwich	le pâté	le beurre	le Bourgueil	....

Vocabulary

Below is a list of vocabulary encountered in this chapter.

à cause de	because of/due to	**gruyère** m	gruyère cheese
addition f	bill	**guide** m	guide
appel m	call	**il faut (falloir)**	one must, one has to
autre chose	something different/else	**immense**	immense, huge
avoir faim	to be hungry	**inviter**	to invite
balade f	stroll	**la prochaine fois**	the next time
beaucoup de	much, plenty, many,	**laisser**	to let
	a lot of	**le matin**	in the morning
beurre m	butter	**marcher**	to walk
café au lait m	coffee w/milk (at home)	**Messieurs, Dames**	formal address of guests
(café) crème m	coffee w/milk (at a café)	**ne … rien**	nothing
chance f	luck	**nouveau**	new
chez moi	at home	**partager**	to share
choix m	choice	**photo** f	photo
citron m	lemon	**plu (plaire)**	pleasing
connu (connaître)	well-known, renowned	**quelque chose**	something
croque-monsieur	toasted ham and cheese	**quiche** f	quiche
	sandwich	**raconter**	to tell, narrate
de bonne heure	early in the day	**rendez-vous** m	meeting, appointment
difficile	difficult	**salade composée** f	mixed salad
en semaine	during the week	**sandwich** m	sandwich
était (être)	was (to be)	**saucisson** m	salami
eu (avoir)	had (to have)	**servir à (sers)**	to serve, to bring, to get
excellent	excellent	**si**	if
faire des photos	to take photos	**tout l'après-midi**	the entire afternoon
faire la queue	to stand in line	**très**	very
fermé	closed	**trop de**	too much
grand	big, large	**vieux**	old

Shopping

Day 10 covers personal pronouns. You will also learn to conjugate verbs ending in *-ayer* (*essayer* - to try). You will learn how to use *ce* to mean this/that, pick up some tips about the French love affair with fashion and you will further boost your vocabulary.

LA MODE...

France is known the world over for its fashion designers: Dior, Chanel, Yves Saint-Laurent, Jean-Paul Gaultier, Christian Lacroix to name but a few. Their **prêt-à-porter** *collections (ready-to-wear collections) are readily available today in many large department stores.*

French conversation: Dans un grand magasin

Au rayon vêtements femmes dans un grand magasin.

Vendeuse: Je peux vous aider ?

Claire: Je voudrais essayer cette robe rouge mais je n'ai pas trouvé ma taille.

Vendeuse: Vous faites du combien ?

Claire: Je fais du 40.

Vendeuse: Attendez, je vais regarder si nous avons encore ce modèle dans votre taille…. Désolée, dans cette couleur je l'ai uniquement en 42.

Claire: Je vais l'essayer quand même.

Dans une cabine d'essayage.

Vendeuse: Ça va ?

Claire: J'hésite !

Vendeuse: Je vous ai apporté un autre modèle très joli en 40 en vert. Vous voulez l'essayer ?

Claire: Elle est bien cette robe, j'aime beaucoup le vert. C'est le même prix ?

Vendeuse: Non, cette robe est un peu plus chère mais la qualité du tissu est meilleure. C'est un autre style aussi, plus élégant. Ça vous plaît ?

Claire: Oui, c'est plus classique. Je vais faire un essai.

5 minutes plus tard.

Claire: Qu'est-ce que vous en pensez ?

Vendeuse: Ça vous va très bien.

Claire: J'ai réfléchi, je la prends.

English conversation: In the department store

In the department store's section for women's wear.

Shop assistant:	Can I help you?
Claire:	I'd like to try on this red dress but couldn't find my size.
Shop assistant:	What size are you?
Claire:	I'm a size 40.
Shop assistant:	Just a moment. I'll check whether we still have that model in your size .... I'm sorry, we have only a 42 left in that colour.
Claire:	I'll try it on anyway.

In the dressing room.

Shop assistant:	Does it fit?
Claire:	I'm not sure.
Shop assistant:	I've brought you another very nice model in green, size 40. Would you like to try it on?
Claire:	That's a nice dress, I like green a lot. Is it the same price?
Shop assistant:	No this dress is a little more expensive, but the material is better quality. It's also a different style, more elegant. Do you like it?
Claire:	Yes, this one is far more classic, I'll try it on.

5 minutes later.

Claire:	What do you think?
Shop assistant:	It really suits you.
Claire:	I've thought about it. I'll take it.

Grammar

Personal pronouns in the accusative

Le, la, les, or l' in front of a vowel or a silent h replace the **direct object** and take their gender and number from it.
For example:

Je cherche *Claire*.	Je *la* cherche.
Je cherche *la secrétaire*.	Je *la* cherche.
Elle essaye *la robe* rouge.	Elle *l'*essaie.
Il essaie le *pull* noir.	Il *l'*essaie.
On cherche *les clés*.	On *les* cherche.
Je cherche *Florent*.	Je *le* cherche.
Je cherche *le professeur*.	Je *le* cherche.
Il cherche *les étudiants*.	Il *les* cherche.

Present tense verbs ending with *-ayer*

essayer (to try out, to try on)
j'essaie
tu essaies
il/elle essaie
nous essayons
vous essayez
ils/elles essaient

perfect tense:

j'ai essayé

Note:
The verb **payer** (to pay) is conjugated in the same way.

Demonstrative determiners

in front of a consonant		
masculine singular	*feminine singular*	*masculine + feminine plural*
ce	cette	ces
ce pull	*cette* robe	*ces* pulls
ce magasin	*cette* vendeuse	*ces* robes

in front of a vowel or silent h		
masculine singular	*feminine singular*	*masculine + feminine plural*
cet	cette	ces
cet hôtel		ces hôtels
cet ami (this male friend)	cette amie (this female friend)	ces amis
		ces amies

Note:
Like adjectives, the gender and number of ce, cet, cette, ces refers to the word they relate to.

Adjectives

Adjectives are determined by the gender and number of the noun that they describe.

un pull noir	a black sweater
des pulls noirs	black sweaters
un pantalon bleu	a pair of blue trousers
une robe bleue	a blue dress
des robes bleues	blue dresses
un foulard vert	a green scarf
une jupe verte	a green skirt
un manteau gris	a grey coat
un chemisier gris	a grey blouse
une chemise grise	a grey (men's) shirt
une voiture noire	a black car
un touriste anglais	an English tourist (male)
une touriste anglaise	an English tourist (female)

If an adjective relates to more than one noun it will take the masculine plural form if the nouns are both masculine and feminine as in **une jupe et un pull bleus** (a blue skirt and a blue sweater).

b) Position
As a general rule the adjective follows the noun. Adjectives that describe a color or nationality always follow the noun.

c) Irregular forms

masculine/singular	blanc (white)	bon (good)	beau (nice)
feminine/singular	blanche	bonne	belle

Adjectives that end in -e in the masculine form, such as **un pull jaune** (a yellow sweater), **un pull rouge** (a yellow sweater), **une jupe jaune** (a yellow skirt), **une jupe rouge** (a red skirt), do not change.

Exercises

Exercise 1

Fill in le, la, l', or les as in the following example. Je cherche la vendeuse. Je *la* cherche.

Le guide cherche les touristes. Il .... cherche. Claire prend la jupe rouge ? Elle ....
prend. Vous connaissez Monsieur Rougier ? Oui, nous .... connaissons. Elles cherchent le
rayon parfumerie ? Oui, elles .... cherchent depuis dix minutes. Tu as l'adresse de Claire ? Oui,
je .... ai. Il connaît le quartier ? Oui, il .... connaît très bien.

Exercise 2

Form sentences using ce, cet, cette or ces.

Example: **Vous aimez (photo *f*)?**   **Vous aimez *cette* photo?**

**Vous aimez (magasin *m*)/(quartier *m*)/(modèle *m*)/(ville *f*)/(hôtel *m*)/(architecture *f*)/
(musique *f*) (café *m*)?**

....

....

....

....

Exercise 3

Match each noun with the appropriate adjective.

1 une robe	**a** françaises	**1** ....
2 des vendeuses	**b** allemande	**2** ....
3 un étudiant	**c** vert	**3** ....
4 des pulls	**d** noire	**4** ....
5 un chemisier (Bluse)	**e** espagnol	**5** ....
6 une touriste	**f** blancs	**6** ....

Exercise 4

Fill in the correct form of the adjective.

1 un pull (bleu) ....

2 une robe (élégant) ....

3 des chemises (*f pl* shirts) (gris) ....

4 un modèle (classique) ....

5 des chaussures (*f pl* shoes) (rouge) ....

6 une voiture (vert) ....

Exercise 5

Match the correct answer to each question.

1	Vous avez ce modèle en rouge ?	**a**	Oui, beaucoup.	**1** ....
2	Vous faites du combien ?	**b**	Non, désolée.	**2** ....
3	C'est le même prix ?	**c**	Ça vous va très bien.	**3** ....
4	Vous voulez l'essayer ?	**d**	Du 38.	**4** ....
5	Ça vous plaît?	**e**	Volontiers (gladly).	**5** ....
6	Ça me va?	**f**	Non, un peu plus cher.	**6** ....

Exercise 6

Complete the sentences.

1	Claire veut .... une robe rouge.	**a**	taille	**1** ....
2	Elle n'a pas trouvé sa	**b**	autre	**2** ....
3	Elle fait .... 40.	**c**	essayer	**3** ....
4	La vendeuse lui apporte un .... modèle.	**d**	l'	**4** ....
5	C'est une robe	**e**	réfléchit	**5** ....
6	Ce modèle est plus	**f**	verte	**6** ....
7	Claire	**g**	du	**7** ....
8	Elle .... achète.	**h**	cher	**8** ....

Vocabulary

Below is a list of vocabulary encountered in this chapter.

aider	to assist, help	**réfléchi**	thought
apporter	to bring	**(réfléchir)**	(to think about/reflect)
aussi	also, too	**regarder**	to look up, check
Ça va? (aller)	Does it fit?	**style** m	style
Ça vous plaît?	Do you like it?	**taille** f	size
ça vous va	it suits you	**tissu** m	fabric, material
(aller)		**très bien**	very good
cabine	dressing room	**trouver**	to find, discover
d'essayage f		**un peu**	a little
ce cet/cette/ces	this/that/these/those	**uniquement**	only
classique	classic(al)	**vert**	green
couleur f	color	**vert** m	(the color) green
désolé(e)	I'm sorry/regrettably	**votre**	your (sing., formal)
élégant	elegant	**botte** f	boot
en 42	in 42 (size)	**bonnet** m	cap, hat
encore	still	**chaussette** f	sock
essai m	try/attempt	**chaussure** f	shoe
essayer	to try out/on	**chemise** f	shirt
étroit	tight	**chemisier** m	blouse
faire du 38	to wear/be size 38	**collant** m	a pair of tights
grand magasin m	department store	**coton** m	cotton
hésiter	to hesitate	**en coton**	made of cotton
meilleur m	better	**court**	short
même	same	**cuir** m	leather
modèle m	model	**écharpe** f	scarf
penser de	to think of	**gant** m	glove
plus cher	more expensive	**imperméable** m	raincoat
prix m	price	**jupe** f	skirt
qualité f	quality	**large**	wide, baggy
quand même	anyway, all the same	**long/longue**	long
rayon m	section, department	**manteau** m	coat

pantalon *m*	*a pair of trousers*
pointure *f*	*shoe size*
pull *m*	*sweater*
sac (à main) *m*	*handbag, backpack*
soutien-gorge	*bra*
veste *f*	*jacket*

Test 2

Work your way around the board. Each correct answer will take you to the next question until you have completed the exercise. Enjoy!

1

Choose one of the two offered solutions and go to the square with the number of your answer.

2

Tout droit jusqu'à ... place!
la ▶8
le ▶15

3

Wrong!

Go back to 5.

8

Correct! continue:
Il n'a pas ... manteau.
du ▶6
de ▶25

9

Wrong!

Go back to 25.

10

Wrong!

Go back to 14.

11

Wrong!

Go back to 29.

16

Well done! Continue:
Tournez ... gauche!
à ▶22
sur ▶18

17

Wrong!

Go back to 22.

18

Wrong!

Go back to 16.

19

Correct!

End of exercise

24

Wrong!

Go back to 12.

25

Very good! Continue:
Tu vas ... musée?
au ▶14
à la ▶9

26

Wrong!

Go back to 30.

27

Well done! Continue:
Claire est ... France.
au ▶23
en ▶12

4

Good! Continue:
Je prends ... lait.
du   ▶20
de la   ▶7

5

Right! Continue:
Il est parti ... Etats-Unis.
en   ▶3
aux   ▶13

6

Wrong!

Go back to 8.

7

Wrong!

Go back to 4.

12

Very good! continue:
Je n'aime pas ... pull.
ce   ▶16
cette   ▶24

13

Correct! Continue:
Il habite ... Londres.
a   ▶21
à   ▶29

14

Very good! Continue:
Je n'aime pas ... beurre.
du   ▶10
le   ▶30

15

Wrong!

Go back to 2.

20

Well done! Continue:
... robe est chère!
Cette   ▶5
Cet   ▶28

21

Wrong!

Go back to 13.

22

Correct! Tu as de
l'argent?
Oui, j'ai.   ▶17
Oui, j'en ai.   ▶19

23

Wrong!

Go back to 27.

28

Wrong!

Go back to 20.

29

Excellent! Continue:
Il téléphone ... hôtel.
à l'   ▶27
au   ▶11

30

Correct! Continue:
Il y a trop ... touristes.
de   ▶4
des   ▶26

day: 11

Dining out

Day 11 discusses eating out in France. You will also learn how to use indirect object pronouns (to me, to you, etc.), to help you make more complex sentences. You will also further increase your vocabulary and you will learn more about French culture.

MEAL DEALS...

*When you go out for a meal in a restaurant and choose to order from the **à la carte** menu, the general assumption is that you will order at least two courses. Many places also do set menus (**menu à prix fixe**) that offer a more limited choice than the **à la carte** menu but at a set price, usually including a starter, main and dessert. During the day, there are often bargains to be had too - look out for signs offering a **formule du midi** - this usally includes a two-course set-menu at a special lunchtime price.*

French conversation: Au restaurant

Claire:	C'est très sympa ici !
Michel:	J'ai découvert ce petit resto avec Caroline il y a un mois.
Caroline:	Ici, on sert des fruits de mer excellents.
Garçon:	Bonsoir Messieurs Dames, vous avez choisi ?
Michel:	Oui, pour moi le menu à e20. Et toi Caroline ?
Caroline:	Je préfère manger à la carte. Comme hors-d'oeuvre des huîtres et après le colin au citron vert. Et toi ?
Claire:	Je ne sais pas quoi prendre. A part les huîtres, qu'est-ce que vous me recommandez ?
Caroline:	Comme entrée, les moules marinière, après, du loup au fenouil, une spécialité provençale. Si tu préfères la viande, je te conseille un steak au poivre aux haricots verts ou bien des côtelettes d'agneau avec un gratin dauphinois.
Claire:	Qu'est-ce que c'est un gratin dauphinois ?
Michel:	C'est un gratin de pommes de terre, une spécialité régionale.
Claire:	Je prends les moules et le steak au poivre. Je peux avoir du gratin dauphinois à la place des haricots ?
Garçon:	Bien sûr, Mademoiselle. Et comme boisson ?
Michel:	Tu aimes le Muscadet ? C'est un vin blanc sec qui va bien avec les fruits de mer.
Claire:	J'adore le Muscadet.
Michel:	Alors une bouteille de Muscadet.

A la fin du repas.

Garçon:	Vous désirez un dessert ?
Caroline:	Oui, deux tartes au citron et une salade de fruits. Claire, tu prends aussi un café après ?
Claire:	Non merci, pas de café pour moi.
Caroline:	Alors deux cafés.

Un peu plus tard.

Michel:	Monsieur, l'addition, s'il vous plaît !
Garçon:	Voilà et des Cointreau offerts par la maison.
Michel:	Merci, c'est gentil.

English conversation: In the restaurant

Claire:	It's very nice here.
Michel:	I discovered this little restaurant a month ago with Caroline.
Caroline:	They serve excellent seafood here.
Waiter:	Good evening, are you ready to order?
Michel:	Yes please, I'll have the set menu for e20. What about you, Caroline?
Caroline:	I prefer eating à la carte. I'll have the oysters as a starter and then the hake with lime. And what about you?
Claire:	I don't know what to have. Besides the oysters, is there anything you would recommend?
Caroline:	The marinated mussels as a starter and then the catfish in fennel, a speciality from Provence. If you prefer meat, I suggest the pepper steak with green beans or lamb chops with gratin dauphinois.
Claire:	What's gratin dauphinois?
Michel:	That's potatoes done in the oven with cream and cheese, a regional speciality.
Claire:	I'll have the mussels and the pepper steak. Can I have the gratin dauphinois as a side dish instead of the green beans?
Waiter:	Of course you can. And what would you like to drink?
Michel:	Do you like Muscadet? It is a dry white wine that goes well with seafood.
Claire:	I love Muscadet!
Michel:	Well then, a bottle of Muscadet.

At the end of the meal.

Waiter:	Would you like a dessert?
Caroline:	Yes please, two lemon tarts and a fruit salad. Claire, would you like coffee afterwards as well?
Claire:	No thanks, no coffee for me.
Caroline:	Two coffees then.
A little later.	
Michel:	The bill please!
Waiter:	Here you are, plus three Cointreaus on the house.
Michel:	Thank you, that's very kind of you.

Grammar

En as a pronoun

En meaning some/of it can be used in multiple instances:

a) En can replace the direct object specifying a quantity. Quantities can be specified by nouns (**un kilo de ...**, **une tasse de ...** etc.), adverbs - **beaucoup de** (plenty of) or **peu de** (little of . . .), the partitive article (**du/de la**) or the indefinite article (**un, une, des**).

b) En abbreviates designations of locations formed with **de**, e.g. **Tu viens de l'aéroport? Oui, j'en viens directement.**

c) En replaces the preposition **de** of certain verbs such as **avoir besoin de** (to need), or **parler de** (to speak of/about). In these cases **en** replaces the preposition **de** which refers only to objects.

Examples:

Tu as des cigarettes ? Oui, j'en ai.
Do you have any cigarettes? Yes I have some.

Tu as des allumettes ? Non, je n'en ai pas.
Do you have matches? No, I don't have any.

Tu as un plan de Paris ? Oui, j'en ai un dans la voiture.
Do you have a map of Paris? Yes, I have one in the car.

Il reste du Muscadet ? Oui, j'en ai encore deux bouteilles.
Is there any Muscadet left? Yes, I still have two bottles.

Tu fais beaucoup de sport ? Oui, j'en fais trois fois par semaine.
Do you do a lot of sport? Yes, three times a week.

Tu viens de l'aéroport ? Oui, j'en viens directement.
Are you coming from the airport? Yes, I'm coming straight from there.

Claire parle de ce voyage ? Oui, elle en parle souvent.
Does Claire talk about her trip? Yes, she talks about it often.

Note:

En is translated by various prepositions and at times not at all, e.g.

Tu as combien de dictionnaires ? *J'en ai deux.*   How many dictionaries do you have? I have two.

Or:

Vous avez du feu ? *Non, je n'en ai pas.*   Do you have a light? No, I don't.

Indirect object pronouns

What do you recommend (to us)?

me/m'	to me
te/t'	to you
vous	to you (plural)
lui	to him, to her, to it
nous	to us
vous	to you
leur	to them

Note:

M' replaces **me** and **t'** replaces **te** in front of a vowel or silent **h**. These pronouns serve as **indirect objects** with verbs that take the preposition **à**, such as **donner à** (to give to), **recommander à** (to recommend to), **conseiller à** (to advise s.o.), **parler à** (to talk to). A number of verbs take an indirect object in French, e.g. **téléphoner à quelqu'un** (to phone s.o.), **demander à quelqu'un** (to ask s.o.).

Note:

Within a sentence the indirect object pronouns are positioned **in front** of the verb:

| Il *me* téléphone. | He calls me (on the phone). |
| Il ne *me* téléphone pas. | He does not call me (on the phone). |

Exercises

Exercise 1

Circle the words en refers to and translate.

1 Tu prends des yaourts ? Oui, j'en prends six.

2 Il reste de l'eau minérale ? Oui, il en reste trois bouteilles.

3 Il y a encore du lait ? Non, il n'y en a plus.

4 Tu as des cigarettes ? Oui, j'en ai encore.

Exercise 2

Match the right answer to the corresponding question.

1 Tu as combien d'enfants ?   a Non, il n'en a pas.

2 Vous avez encore du lait ?   b Oui, j'en prends un kilo.

3 Il fait du sport ?   c J'en ai trois.

4 Il a un plan du métro ?   d Non, il n'en fait jamais.

5 Tu prends des oranges ?   e Oui, j'en ai un litre.

1......... 2......... 3......... 4......... 5.........

Exercise 3

Using the following example, complete the sentences using lui or leur.

Paul donne un plan à Caroline.   Il *lui* donne un plan.

1 Claire parle de ses vacances à Luis. Elle .... parle de ses vacances.

2 John et Mary téléphonent au professeur de français. Ils .... téléphonent.

3 Caroline recommande le loup au fenouil à Claire et à Michel. Elle .... recommande le loup au fenouil.

4 Miko demande l'heure à Luis. Elle .... demande l'heure.

5 Claire donne du chocolat aux enfants. Elle .... donne du chocolat.

Exercise 4

What do you say if you . . .

1 . . . like oysters?

    a J'adore les huîtres.

    b Je déteste les huîtres

2 . . . want to have something recommended?

    a Qu'est-ce que vous avez ?

    b Qu'est-ce que vous me recommandez ?

3 . . . order the set menu for €20?

    a Pour moi le menu €20.

    b Pour moi le menu à €20.

4 . . . want to order a pepper steak?

    a Un steak au poivre, s'il vous plaît.

    b Un steak poivre, s'il vous plaît.

5 . . . want to pay the bill?

    a Payer, s'il vous plaît !

    b Monsieur, l'addition, s'il vous plaît !

1 .... **2** .... **3** .... **4** .... **5** ....

Exercise 5

One word in each line is out of place. Which one?

1 le colin	ll loup de mer	les huîtres	le steak
2 les haricots	le dessert	le fenouil	la salade
3 la viande	le gratin	la côtelette	le jambon
4 manger	déjeuner	dîner	parler

1 .... **2** .... **3** .... **4** ....

Vocabulary

Below is a list of vocabulary encountered in this chapter.

addition f	bill, check		**légume** m	vegetable
agneau m	lamb		**loup de mer** m	sea bass
à la marinière	marinated, pickled		**manger**	to eat
à la place	instead		**menu** m	set menu
à part	except		**mois** m	month
A ta (votre) santé ! Cheers!		**moule** f	mussel
bien sûr	of course, obviously		**offert par la**	on the house
boisson f	drink		**maison**	
bœuf m	beef		**petit**	small, little
carotte f	carrot		**petit pois** m	pea
carte f	menu		**pintade** f	guinea-fowl
choisir	to choose		**plus tard**	later
citron m	lemon		**poivre** m	pepper
citron vert m	lime		**poisson** m	fish
colin m	hake		**pomme de terre** f	potato
comme	as, like		**porc** m	pork
conseiller à	to advise		**poulet** m	chicken
crevette f	shrimp		**provençal**	from Provence
découvert	discovered		**quoi**	what
dernier	last		**recommander à**	to recommend to
désirer	to wish for, desire		**régional**	regional
dessert m	dessert		**repas** m	meal, food
dîner	to dine, eat dinner		**restaurant** m	restaurant
entrée f	starter/appetizer		**rôti** m	roast
excellent	excellent		**salade de fruits** f	fruit salad
fenouil m	fennel		**sec**	dry
fin f	end		**souvent**	often
fruits de mer m pl	seafood		**spécialité** f	speciality
glace f	ice cream		**steak** m	steak
gratin	gratin potatoes		**tarte** f	tart
dauphinois m			**un peu**	a little
haricot m	bean		**viande** f	meat
hors-d'œuvre m	starter/ appetizer		**vin blanc** m	white wine
huître f	oyster			

day:12

At the station

Day 12 covers all the ways that you can ask questions. You will also learn how to talk about things belonging to someone using possessive determiners (my, yours, his, etc.). Finally, you will discover more about traveling by train in France and you will further expand your vocabulary.

RAIL TRANSPORT ...

*France has a fast, efficient rail network operated by the SNCF. The acclaimed TGV is its high-speed, long-distance train. Tickets usually need to be reserved in advance but it is possible to get reduced fares at the last minute if your plans are flexible. Before boarding any train, tickets must be stamped (**composter** to stamp) at the yellow machines at the top of the platforms.*

French conversation: A la gare

Claire est à la gare de Lyon au guichet grandes lignes.

Claire: Bonjour Monsieur. Je voudrais deux billets pour Grenoble, s'il vous plaît.

Employé: Aller simple ou aller et retour ?

Claire: Aller et retour, deuxième classe.

Employé: Vous prenez le TGV de quelle heure ?

Claire: Celui de 10 heures 05, jeudi prochain.

Employé: Voulez-vous des places fumeurs ou non-fumeurs ?

Claire: Non-fumeurs, près de la fenêtre, si possible.

Employé: Voilà vos réservations. Vous avez les places 28 et 30 voiture 12. N'oubliez pas de composter vos billets et vos réservations avant le départ.

Claire: A quelle heure on arrive à Grenoble ?

Employé: Vous arrivez à Grenoble à 13 heures 11.

Claire: Est-ce qu'il y a encore une correspondance pour Chamrousse ?

Employé: Attendez, je vais vous dire ça tout de suite ... Voilà, il y a un service de cars SNCF Grenoble Chamrousse. Vous en avez toutes les heures jusqu'à 21 heures.

English conversation: At the train station

Claire is at the gare de Lyon at the ticket counter for long distance journeys.

Claire: Hi. I'd like two tickets to Grenoble, please.

Railway employee: One way or return (roundtrip)?

Claire: Return tickets, second class.

Railway employee: Which TGV do you want to take?

Claire: The one at 10:05 next Thursday.

Railway employee: Do you want smoking or non-smoking seats?

Claire: Non-smoking and near the window, if possible.

Railway employee: Here are your reservations. You have seats 28 and 30, carriage 12. Don't forget to stamp your tickets and reservations before departure.

Claire: What time do we arrive in Grenoble?

Railway employee: You'll arrive in Grenoble at 1:11 p.m.

Claire: Is there also a connection to Chamrousse?

Railway employee: One moment please, I'll tell you right away... There is a SNCF bus service from Grenoble to Chamrousse that runs every hour until 9 p.m.

Grammar

Questions

a) a statement is turned into a question through **intonation** (see Day 3)

Vous prenez le TGV ?	Are you taking the TGV?

b) questions formed with **est-ce que** (see Day 6)

Est-ce que vous prenez le TGV ?

c) questions formed by **inversion**

Prenez-vous le TGV ?

Questions formed by inversion are made by placing the verb before the subject pronoun and hyphenating the two. In the third person singular form of verbs, **t** is added to separate two vowels coming together, e.g.:

Où va-t-il ?	Where is he going?

If the verb's subject is a noun, the subject of the verb must be repeated using a pronoun, e.g.:

Le train pour Grenoble est-il déjà en gare ?	Has the train to Grenoble already entered the station?

There are three different ways of forming questions with an **interrogative pronoun** (e.g. où/where (to), comment/how, quand/when etc.).

Tu vas *où* ?	**Tu vas *comment* ?**	**Elle part *quand* ?**
Où **est-ce que tu vas ?**	*Comment* **est-ce que tu vas ?**	*Quand* **est-ce qu'elle part ?**
Où **vas-tu ?**	*Comment* **vas-tu ?**	*Quand* **part-elle ?**

Possessive determiners

Possessive determiners agree both in gender and number with the noun to which they refer.

Je cherche *mon* billet.	I am looking for my ticket.
Je cherche *ma* valise.	I am looking for my suitcase.
J'attends *mon* ami/amie.	I am waiting for my (male/female) friend.
Tu as *ton* billet ?	Have you got your ticket?
Tu cherches *ta* valise ?	Are you looking for your suitcase?
Tu attends *ton* amie ?	Are you waiting for your friend?
Elle cherche *son* billet.	She's looking for her ticket.
Il cherche *son* billet.	He's looking for his ticket.
Nous cherchons *notre* plan.	We are looking for our map.
Vous cherchez *votre* billet ?	Are you looking for your ticket?
Vous cherchez *votre* hôtel ?	Are you looking for your hotel?
Ils cherchent *leur* clé.	They are looking for their key.
Ils cherchent *leurs* enfants.	They are looking for their children.

singular		singular		plural	
masculine		*feminine*		*masculine+feminine*	
mon	my	ma	my	mes	my
ton	your	ta	your	tes	your
son	his/her/its	sa	his/her/its	ses	his/her/its
notre	our	notre	our	nos	our
votre	your	votre	your	vos	your
leur	their	leur	their	leurs	their

Note: **Mon, ton, son** are placed in front of feminine nouns beginning with a **vowel** as in **mon amie**, my (female) friend.

Exercises

Exercise 1

Use the following example to rephrase the questions below.

Est-ce que vous aimez les voyages ? *Aimez-vous les voyages ?*

1 Est-ce que vous prenez le train pour Grenoble ?

....

2 Est-ce que vous allez à Chamrousse ?

....

3 Est-ce que vous prenez un taxi ?

....

4 Est-ce que vous avez un hôtel ?

....

5 Est-ce que vous connaissez ce restaurant ?

....

6 Est-ce que vous faites du ski de fond ?

....

7 Est-ce que vous restez une semaine ?

....

8 Est-ce que vous êtes professeur d'anglais ?

....

9 Est-ce que vous avez un journal (a newspaper) ?

....

Exercise 2

Follow the example below and fill in the appropriate possessive determiner.

Vous avez ... billet ?   *Vous avez votre billet ?*

Vous attendez .... amis ? Tu cherches .... journal ? Je cherche ....

cigarettes. Il a garé .... voiture rue de Rivoli. Elle cherche .... place dans le train.

Elle attend .... ami. Il téléphone à .... secrétaire. Je cherche .... hôtel.

Tu prends .... petit déjeuner à quelle heure ? Ils cherchent .... réservations.

Exercise 3

Qu'est-ce que vous avez oublié dans le train?   **What did you leave on the train?**

J'ai oublié ... journal (m). J'ai oublié *mon* journal.

J'ai oublié .... valise *(f)*, ... bagages *(m pl)*, ... sac *(m)*, ...

passeport *(m)*, ... lunettes *(f pl) (glasses)*, ... iPad *(m)*.

Exercise 4

Fill in the appropriate possessive determiner.

1 Claire attend .... amis au café.

2 Miko a oublié .... sac dans le métro.

3 Claire n'a pas composté .... billet à la gare.

4 Luis cherche .... clés de voiture.

5 Il a garé .... voiture rue de Fleurus.

6 Miko et Luis ont rendez-vous à la Tartine, c'est .... café préféré.

7 Caroline et Michel Rougier accompagnent .... enfants à la gare.

8 Claire a invité .... professeur à manger des crêpes.

9 Caroline aime le vert, c'est ....couleur préférée.

10 Ils habitent dans le quartier ? Je n'ai pas .... adresse.

11 Miko cherche le numéro de .... sa place.

12 Luis prend toujours du Bourgueil, c'est .... vin préféré.

Exercise 5

Translate the following text into French:

I would like a ticket to Paris, please. One way or return? Return, second class. Here is your ticket, you have seat 10, carriage 13. What time do I arrive? At 10 p.m.

....

....

....

....

....

....

....

Vocabulary

Below is a list of vocabulary encountered in this chapter.

aller retour m	return/ round trip ticket	**non-fumeur**	non-smoking
aller simple m	one way (ticket)	**oublier**	to forget
arrivée f	arrival	**place (assise)** f	seat
banlieue f	suburb	**pour Grenoble**	to Grenoble
billet m	ticket	**première classe**	first class
celui de	that at	**quai** m	platform
composter	here: to stamp/validate	**réservation** f	reservation
correspondance f	connection	**service de cars** m	bus connection
consigne f	left luggage	**si possible**	if possible
couchette f	sleeping car	**SNCF** f	French state-run railway
couloir m	corridor	**tout de suite**	immediately
départ m	departure	**toutes les heures**	every hour
deuxième classe	second class	**train** m	train
employé m	employee	**voie** f	track
fenêtre f	window	**voiture** f	train carriage
fumer	to smoke	**wagon-restaurant** m	dining car restaurant
fumeur m	smoker		
grandes lignes	long distance f pl		
guichet m	ticket counter		
jeudi prochain	next Thursday		
journeys horaire m	timetable		

The ski trip

Day 13 teaches you the days of the week, the months and dates. You will also learn about one of the nation's most favorite pasttimes - skiing, as well as pick up some useful tips about false friends - words that have an English equivalent but that do not mean the same thing in French!

OOPS...

*Watch out for the 'false friends' - words that have an English equivalent but that do not mean the same as they do in French. Some common examples include: **le car** (the bus), **la cave** (cellar, basement), **la conférence** (lecture), **la librairie** (bookstore), **le magasin** (store), **le médecin** (doctor), **la monnaie** (change/coins), **une prune** (plum), **un raisin** (grape), **sale** (dirty), **affaire** (business), **assister à** (to attend something).*

French conversation: Weekend au ski

Vendredi en gare de Grenoble.

Claire: Pardon Monsieur, est-ce qu'il y a un car pour
Chamrousse ?
Employé: C'est le car qui s'arrête devant la gare. Dépêchez-vous, il va bientôt
partir !

A Chamrousse. Claire et Miko cherchent une chambre d'hôtel.

Claire: Bonjour Madame, vous avez une chambre pour deux personnes ?
Réceptioniste: Vous avez de la chance! J'en ai encore une de libre. D'habitude en
pleine saison, tout est complet ! Et si vous voulez faire du ski je loue
aussi du matériel. Profitez-en! La neige est excellente sur les pistes
du moins en ce moment !
Claire: Super! Miko, tu sais bien skier ?
Miko: J'ai déjà fait deux stages avec un moniteur. Je me débrouille, mais
pour les pistes noires, ne compte pas sur moi !
Claire: Moi, j'adore le hors piste. Allons-y. Au fait, c'est possible d'acheter
un forfait pour le weekend ?
Réceptioniste: Ah oui! Les forfaits sont à la journée et ils coûtent 30 euros par
personne, toutes les remontées mécaniques comprises. Vous
pouvez ausssi prendre un forfait horaire, mais c'est plus cher. Mais
il est encore tôt, vous avez toute la journée devant vous et il fait un
temps superbe. Amusez-vous bien! La météo prévoit des chutes de
neige pour ce week-end !

English conversation: Skiing over the weekend

Friday, at the train station in Grenoble.

Claire: Excuse me, sir, is there a bus to Chamrousse?
Railway
employee: There's a bus that stops outside the station. Hurry up,
it's going to leave soon.

In Chamrousse. Claire and Miko are looking for a hotel room.

Claire: Good afternoon. Do you have a room for two?

Receptionist:	You're in luck! I still have one vacancy. Normally everything is booked up during the peak season! And if you want to go skiing I also hire (rent out) the equipment. Make the most of it! The snow on the slopes is superb right now.
Claire:	Great! Miko, can you ski well?
Miko:	I've completed two courses with an instructor. I can manage, but don't count on me when it comes to the black slopes!
Claire:	I love to ski off-piste! Let's go! By the way, is it possible to buy a ski-pass for the weekend?
Receptionist:	Sure! The ski passes are good for one day and cost 30 euros per person, which includes all the lifts. You can also buy an hourly ticket but that's more expensive. But it's still early, you have the whole day ahead of you and the weather is wonderful. Enjoy yourselves! The weather report forecasts snow for the weekend.

Grammar

Days of the week

The names of the days of the week, months and seasons are all masculine.

lundi	Monday
mardi	Tuesday
mercredi	Wednesday
jeudi	Thursday
vendredi	Friday
samedi	Saturday
dimanche	Sunday

Vous arrivez quand? Dimanche.	When do you arrive? On Sunday.
Vous arrivez quand? Le 28 juin.	When do you arrive? On the 28th of June.
J'ai rendez-vous le mardi 12 octobre.	I have a meeting on Tuesday, the 12th of October.
Je suis en vacances en juin or au mois de juin.	I am on holiday in June.
Vous restez combien de temps à Lyon?	How long will you be staying in Lyon?
Trois jours, du 2 au 4 mai.	For three days, from the 2nd to the 4th of May.

Months

janvier	January
février	February
mars	March
avril	April
mai	May
juin	June
juillet	July
août	August
septembre	September
octobre	October
novembre	November
décembre	December

The first day of the month is indicated by an ordinal number (**premier**). All the other days of the month take their respective cardinal numbers. When writing letters, you should always follow the format:

city, the day/month/year   e.g. **Paris, le 12 octobre 1995**

When talking about a certain day, you would say:

Aujourd'hui c'est le 1er (premier) mai.	Today is the 1st of May.
Aujourd'hui or nous sommes le 3 (trois) juin.	Today is the 12th of April/3rd of June.

Verbs

partir (to depart, to leave)

present tense:

je pars	nous partons
tu pars	vous partez
il/elle/on part	ils/elles partent

perfect tense:

je suis parti(e)
tu es parti(e)

Reflexive verbs

se renseigner (to ask for information, to find out)

present tense:

je me renseigne	nous nous renseignons
tu te renseignes	vous vous renseignez
il/elle/on se renseigne	ils/elles se renseignent

Note:
Me, te, se become m', t', s' before a vowel or a silent h, e.g. s'amuser (to enjoy oneself): je m'amuse, tu t'amuses, il/elle s'amuse etc.
Not every French reflexive verb is reflexive in English, e.g. s'appeler (to call, to be named), se promener (to go for a walk), se débrouiller (to cope, to get by).

imperative	
Renseigne-toi!	Find out yourself!
Renseignez-vous!	Find out yourself!/Find out yourselves!

Note: Te becomes toi in the imperative.

Exercises

Exercise 1

Using the following example, write out the dates of birth in full.

25.6. (Gérard) Le vingt-cinq juin, c'est l'anniversaire de Gérard.

Gérard's birthday is on the 25th of June.

1 1. 20.5. (Caroline) ....

2 11.11. (Miko) ....

3 8.3. (Luis) ....

4 1.4. (Claire) ....

5 12.10. (Michel) ....

Exercise 2

Fill in the correct endings of partir in the present tense.

Je (partir) .... en Angleterre au mois de septembre. Quand est-ce que vous

(partir) ....? Nous (partir)................. un peu plus tard en octobre. Est-ce que Claire

(partir) .... avec vous? Je ne sais pas. Et toi, tu (partir) .... avec Luis et Abel ?

Non, ils (partir) .... une semaine avant moi, je les rejoins à Londres.

Exercise 3

Fill in the correct form of the reflexive verb.

1 Je (se renseigner) .... sur les prix des hôtels.

2 Tu (se renseigner) .... sur les bus pour Chamrousse.

3 Vous (se renseigner) .... sur les prix des forfaits.

4 Elle (se débrouiller) .... bien (gut) en français.

5 Il (s'appeler) .... Luis.

6 Les enfants (s'amuser) .... bien au ski.

Exercise 4

Complete the sentences.

1 Claire et Miko sont .... à Chamrousse.   **a** neige

2 A Grenoble elles ont pris le ....   **b** skis

3 Elles cherchent une .... pour 2 personnes.   **c** sait

4 Claire .... skier sur les pistes noires.   **d** car

5 Miko ne .... pas bien faire du ski.   **e** moniteur

6 Elle veut prendre des cours avec un ....   **f** arrivées

7 Il y a beaucoup de .... à Chamrousse.   **g** chambre

8 On peut louer des .... à l'hôtel.   **h** veut

1 ....   **2** ....   **3** ....   **4** ....   **5** ....   **6** ....   **7** ....   **8** ....

Exercise 5

One word in each line is out of place. Which one?

1	SNCF	le train	la voiture	le car
2	la piste	le moniteur	le ski	la chambre
3	coûter	réserver	louer	chercher
4	le forfait	la journée	le mois	la semaine
5	lundi	août	jeudi	mardi
6	s'arrêter	se renseigner	s'amuser	visiter

1............. 2............. 3............. 4............. 5............. 6.............

Exercise 6

Translate the following text:

Excuse me, is there a coach to Deux-Alpes? There is a coach that leaves (partir) at 10 o'clock. Do you have a single room (pour une personne or individuelle). I am sorry, (je regrette), we're fully booked! Where can I hire skis? Can we buy a ski-pass for the weekend?

....

....

....

....

....

....

....

Vocabulary

Below is a list of vocabulary encountered in this chapter.

acheter	to buy	**neige** f	snow
au fait	by the way, in fact	**par personne**	per person
au ski	skiing	**piste** f	ski run/slope
bus m	(city) bus	**pleine saison** f	peak season
car m	coach, long-distance bus	**plus cher**	expensive
chambre	(hotel) room	**possible**	possible
(d'hôtel) f		**prévoir (prévoit)**	to forecast/predict
chance f	luck	**qui**	who (relative pronoun)
chute de neige f	snowfall	**réceptionniste** f	receptionist
complet	fully booked (up)	**remontée**	ski lift
compris	inclusive	**mécanique** f	
coûter	to cost	**s'amuser**	to have fun
d'habitude	normally	**s'arrêter**	to stop o.s.
du moins	at least	**se débrouiller**	to cope/get by/manage
en ce moment	at the moment	**se dépêcher**	to hurry up
excellent	excellent	**si**	if, whether
forfait m	ski-pass	**ski** m	ski
horaire	here: per hour	**faire du ski**	to go skiing
il fait un temps	the weather is superb	**stage** m	course; internship
superbe		**tôt**	early
journée f	day	**tout** m	all
libre	free	**tous** m pl	all
location f	rental	**toute** f sing.	all
louer	to hire /rent	**toutes** f pl	all
matériel m	gear, equipment	**vendredi**	Friday
météo f	weather report	**weekend** m	weekend
moniteur	(skiing) instructor		
(de ski) m			

A chance encounter

Day 14 covers some more essential verbs such as *voir* (to see), *lire* (to read), *acheter* (to buy). You will learn how to use *qui* to mean who, which or that. You will also learn how to compare things and people. Finally, check your progress with the fun game on page 144.

THE PRESS...

*The main national dailies are **Le Monde** (good for a liberal overview of political and economic news), the more conservative **Le Figaro**, and the left-wing papers **Libération** and **L'Humanité**. **Le Point**, **Le Nouvel Observateur** and **L'Express** are the major weekly news publications. International newspapers and magazines are available in the bigger cities also, although they will usually circulate a day or two later than in their country of origin.*

French conversation: Rencontre dans le TGV

Le train démarre. Claire est assise à côté de Denis plongé dans la lecture de son journal.

Claire:	Excusez-moi, je vois que vous lisez »Le Figaro«, je n'ai pas eu le temps de l'acheter à la gare. Je peux avoir les pages des petites annonces ?
Denis:	Pourquoi les petites annonces? Vous cherchez du travail ?
Claire:	Oui, je voudrais trouver un stage dans une agence de communication à Paris.
Denis:	En ce moment ce n'est pas facile, mais j'ai peut-être un tuyau pour vous.
Claire:	Vous êtes sérieux ?
Denis:	Toujours, mais d'abord je me présente, je m'appelle Denis Moisson, je travaille à Paris dans une agence de communication. Mon patron cherche quelqu'un qui parle anglais et aussi un peu allemand pour organiser des rencontres avec nos clients européens. Ça vous intéresse ?
Claire:	Mais c'est exactement ce que j'aimerais faire. Je cherche depuis trois semaines et je n'ai rien trouvé! Je suis anglaise, je parle allemand couramment et j'ai une formation de secrétaire.
Denis:	Alors, il faut tenter votre chance. Tenez, voilà ma carte avec mon numéro au bureau. Attendez, je vous écris aussi mon numéro de téléphone personnel, ... mon adresse ... Encore plus simple, je vous invite demain soir chez moi à l'apéritif pour discuter de votre candidature. Vous acceptez ?
Claire:	Pourquoi pas, vers quelle heure ?
Denis:	Je rentre du bureau vers 7 heures. Ça vous va ?
Claire:	Entendu !

English conversation: Encounter on the TGV

The train pulls away. Claire is sitting next to Denis, who is absorbed in his newspaper.

Claire:	Excuse me, I see you are reading the "Figaro". I had no time to buy one at the station. Could I have the pages with the classified ads?
Denis:	Why the ads? Are you looking for a job?
Claire:	Yes, I would like to do an internship with an advertising agency in Paris.
Denis:	That is not easy at the moment, but I might have a tip for you.
Claire:	Are you serious?
Denis:	Of course, but let me introduce myself first: I am Denis Moisson and I work for an advertising agency in Paris. My boss is looking for someone who speaks English and also a little German to organize meetings between our European customers. Are you interested?
Claire:	That's exactly what I would like to do. I've been looking for the last three weeks and haven't found anything yet. I am English, but I am fluent in German and I'm a trained secretary.
Denis:	Well then, you should try your luck. Here's my card with my telephone number at the office. Wait a minute, I'll also give you my private number,… my address … Even better, I'll invite you for a drink tomorrow evening at my place and we can discuss your application. Do you accept?
Claire:	Why not, at what time?
Denis:	I'll be back from the office at about 7 o'clock. Is that all right for you?
Claire:	Of course it is!

Grammar

Verbs

voir (to see)	lire (to read)	acheter (to buy)
present tense:		
je vois	je lis	j'achète
tu vois	tu lis	tu achètes
il/elle/on voit	il/elle/on lit	il/elle/on achète
nous voyons	nous lisons	nous achetons
vous voyez	vous lisez	vous achetez
ils/elles voient	ils/elles lisent	ils/elles achètent

perfect tense:		
j'ai vu	j'ai lu	j'ai acheté

The relative pronoun qui

The relative pronoun **qui** (who/which/that) is always the subject in relative clauses. It can relate to persons as well as to objects.

C'est le bus *qui* part à 9 heures.
That's the bus which leaves at 9 o'clock.
C'est Claire *qui* achète le journal.
That's Claire who is buying the newspaper.
les touristes *qui* partent à 9 heures
the tourists who are departing at 9 o'clock

Comparative and superlative

comparative:	
a) plus ... que ...	
Il est *plus* grand *que* Paul.	He is taller than Paul.
Tu es *plus* grande *que* Miko.	You are taller than Miko.
Elle parle *plus que* Denis.	She speaks more than Denis.
b) moins ... que	
Il est *moins* sportif *qu'*elle.	He is less athletic than she is.
Elle est *moins* triste *que* moi.	She is not as sad as I am.
Il fume *moins que* Luis.	He smokes less than Luis.

superlative:

a) le plus, la plus, les plus

Elle lit *le plus*.	She reads the most.
le plus simple	the easiest
C'est *le plus* grand.	He is the tallest.
C'est *la plus* intelligente.	She is the smartest.
les hôtels *les plus* chers	the most expensive hotels

b) le moins, la moins, les moins

C'est *le moins* riche.	He is the poorest.
C'est *la moins* grande.	She is the smallest.
les hôtels *les moins* chers	the cheapest hotels

Exercises

Exercise 1

Fill in the correct form of the verb in the present tense.

Qu'est-ce que tu (lire) .... comme journal? »Le Figaro«, et toi ? Moi, je

(lire) ....»Le Monde«. Vous (acheter) .... les billets de train jeudi ? Non, je

les (acheter) .... aujourd'hui. Est-ce que vous (voir) .... Claire ce week-end ?

Oui, je la (voir) .... à Grenoble. Nous (partir)............... faire du ski.

Exercise 2

Using the following example, form sentences with the relative pronoun.

e.g. C'est Miko. Elle achète le journal. C'est Miko qui achète le journal.

Miko aime/déteste . . .

1 C'est Claire. Elle est assise à côté de Denis.

....

2 C'est Denis. Il travaille dans une agence à Paris.

....

3 C'est le TGV pour Grenoble. Il part à 10 heures.

....

4 C'est la patronne de l'hôtel. Elle loue des skis.

....

5 C'est le restaurant japonais. Il n'est pas cher.

....

Exercise 3

Follow the example to form comparisons.

Paris/York/+ grand: *Paris est plus grand que York.*

York/Paris/ − grand: *York est moins grand que Paris.*

1 une chambre à Paris/une chambre à Chamrousse/+ chère

....

2 une chambre à Chamrousse/une chambre à Paris/− chère

....

3 l'hôtel à Tokyo/l'hôtel à Paris/+ cher

....

4 l'hôtel à Paris/l'hôtel à Tokyo/− cher

....

5 l'Europe/l'Afrique/+ riche

....

6 l'Afrique/l'Europe/− riche

....

7 la lecture du Figaro/la lecture du Monde/+ facile

....

8 la lecture du Monde/la lecture du Figaro/− facile

....

Exercise 4

Put these sentences into the perfect tense.

1 Le train part à 10 heures.

....

2 Je rencontre Miko dans le TGV.

....

3 Elle achète le journal.

....

4 On lit les petites annonces du Figaro.

....

5 Elle voit Luis lundi.

....

Exercise 5

Translate this passage into French:

I have been looking for work (du travail) for (depuis) three weeks. I read the classified ads. I have a tip for you. My boss is looking for a secretary who speaks English and German. Are you interested? I'll invite you for a drink at my place tomorrow (demain). At what time? I work until (jusqu'à) 7 o'clock; come at 8 o'clock.

....
....
....
....
....
....
....

Vocabulary

Below is a list of vocabulary encountered in this chapter.

accepter	to accept	**lire**	to read
acheter	to buy	**mais**	but
adresse personnelle f	private address	**numéro de téléphone** m	telephone number
agence de communication f	advertising agency	**organiser**	to organize
		patron m	boss
apéritif m	drink, apéritif	**petites annonces** f pl	classified (small) ads
aussi	also		
avoir le temps de (+ infinitive)	to have time to	**peut-être**	maybe
		plongé dans	absorbed in
ça	that	**plus simple**	more simply, even better
Ça vous va?	Is that alright for you?	**pour** (+ infinitive)	in order to
candidature f	application	**pourquoi pas**	why not
carte de visite f	(business) card	**pourquoi**	why
chance f	luck	**quelqu'un**	someone
chez moi	at my place	**qui**	who/which/that
client m	client, customer	**rencontrer**	to meet
couramment	fluent	**rentrer du bureau**	to return home from the office
dans	in		
démarrer	to start up, pull away	**se présenter**	to introduce oneself
discuter de	to discuss, speak about	**semaine** f	week
en ce moment	at the moment	**sérieux**	serious
entendu	all right, of course	**simple**	simple, easy
être assis	to sit	**tenez**	here ...
facile	easy	**tenter**	to try
rencontre f	meeting, encounter	**toujours**	always
intéresser	to interest	**travail** m	work, job
inviter	to invite	**travailler**	to work,
j'aimerais	I'd like to	**trouver**	to find
jeune homme m	young man	**tuyau** m	tip, hint
journal m	newspaper	**vers**	around, towards
lecture f	reading		

day:15

Making calls

Day 15 helps you to make phone calls in French. You will also learn how to form the future tense (*futur simple*) of verbs ending in -*er*, as well as the irregular but essential verbs *être*, *avoir* and *aller*. Discover more about working in France.

ALLO...

When you first make your call, start your introduction with allô or bonjour before you give your name and the name of the company on whose behalf you are calling (e.g. Anne de la société X or simply société X). You can also name the job you have in your company such as responsable du service après-vente (in charge of customer service) or just your department i.e. service marketing.

French conversation: Coup de fil à l'agence

Secrétaire:	Agence Charrain, bonjour.
Claire:	Allô, ici Claire Dietz, j'aimerais parler au directeur de l'agence, Monsieur Charrain.
Secrétaire:	C'est à quel sujet ?
Claire:	J'ai rencontré Monsieur Moisson qui travaille chez vous. Il m'a dit que vous cherchez une stagiaire qui parle anglais et allemand. Je voudrais poser ma candidature.
Secrétaire:	Laissez-moi votre numéro de téléphone. Je ne peux pas déranger Monsieur Charrain, il est en réunion. Je lui laisse votre message, il vous rappellera à 5 heures.

5 heures, Monsieur Charrain appelle Claire.

Claire:	Allo? ... Oui, c'est moi, bonjour Monsieur... Oui, c'est exact, je suis anglaise, ... Oui, je parle allemand.
M. Charrain:	J'aimerais vous rencontrer pour discuter des conditions de stage. Vous êtes libre jeudi après-midi à 3 heures ?
Claire:	Oui, je n'ai rien de prévu.
M. Charrain:	Très bien, rendez-vous donc jeudi à 3 heures. N'oubliez pas de me faire un petit C.V. avec votre formation et vos expériences professionnelles. Au revoir, Mademoiselle.

English conversation: Calling the agency

Secretary:	Charrain Agency, good morning.
Claire:	Hello, this is Claire Dietz, I would like to speak to Mr. Charrain, the director of the agency.
Secretary:	About what?
Claire:	I met Mr. Moisson, who works with you, and he told me that you are looking for an intern who speaks English and German. I would like to apply.
Secretary:	Leave me your phone number. I can't interrupt Mr. Charrain right now; he's in a meeting. I will give him your message and he'll get in touch with you at 5 o'clock.

5 p.m., Mr. Charrain calls Claire.

Claire:	Hello? ... Yes, that's me, good afternoon ... Yes, that's correct, I'm English ... Yes, I speak German.
M. Charrain:	I'd like to meet you to discuss the terms of the intern-ship. Have you got time on Thursday at 3 p.m.?
Claire:	Yes, I have no plans for then.
M. Charrain:	Good, then we'll meet on Thursday at 3 p.m. Don't forget to bring a short CV showing your education and work experience. Goodbye.

Grammar

Making a phone call

1. How to answer the phone:

a) Allô, ici Claire Dietz de la société X (company X), je voudrais parler à Monsieur/Madame X.
If you don't know the extention number (**le numéro de poste**) of Monsieur/Madame X, and cannot dial the person directly, or if the other party does not pick up the phone, you'll be transferred.
b) Allô? ... Bonjour Madame/Monsieur, Claire Dietz de la société X.
You were able to dial the extension directly.

2. How will your call be answered?

a) Allô, bonjour, ici l'agence Charrain.

b) Oui, c'est à quel sujet ?	About what?
c) Bonjour Madame/Monsieur, que puis-je faire pour vous ?	What can I do for you?

In **a)** the central switchboard (**le standard**) (or with smaller companies, the secretary) this will be the greeting. In **b)** you are being asked why you are phoning. In **c)** the other person on the phone wants to know how they can help you.

3. You are unable to reach your associate, because ...

a) ... he/she is not there:

Monsieur/Madame ... est absent/e.	Mr./Ms. ... (He/she) is not there.
Monsieur/Madame ... est en voyage d'affaires.	Mr./Ms. ... (He / she) is on a business trip.

b) ... he/she is temporarily unavailable:

Il/elle est en réunion/en conférence.	He/she is in a meeting.
C'est occupé.	The phone is busy.
Il/elle parle sur l'autre ligne.	He/she is speaking on the other line.

4. You are being put through:

Je vous passe Monsieur/Madame ...	I'll put you through!
Ne quittez pas !	Hold the line!

5. You are being put off until later:

Vous pouvez le/la joindre à 7 heures.	You can reach him/her at 7 o'clock.
Vous voulez rappeler ?	Would you like to call back?
Il/elle peut vous rappeler ?	Can he / she call you back?
Vous voulez laisser un message ?	Would you like to leave a message?

The future tense: verbs ending in -*er*

To form the future tense or **futur simple** of verbs ending in -**er**, you simply take the infinitive of the verb and add the endings in the table below. **Chercher** is given as an example.

verbs ending in -ir	ending	chercher (to look for)
je/j' ...	-ai	je chercherai
tu ...	-as	tu chercheras
il/elle ...	-a	il/elle cherchera
nous	-ons	nous chercherons
vous ...	-ez	vous chercherez
ils/elles ...	-ont	ils/elles chercheront

The future tense: irregular verbs

être	avoir	aller
je serai	j'aurai	j'irai
tu seras	tu auras	tu iras
il/elle sera	il/elle aura	il/elle ira
nous serons	nous aurons	nous irons
vous serez	vous aurez	vous irez
ils/elles seront	ils/elles auront	ils/elles iront

Exercises

Exercise 1

What do you say if you ...

1 ... answer the phone?	**a**	Campell.	**1** ....
	b	Allô, ici Don Campell.	
	c	Allô, Campell.	
2 ... want to speak to Madame Gaume?	**a**	Je veux Madame Gaume.	**2** ....
	b	Je voudrais parler à Madame Gaume.	
	c	La Gaume, s'il vous plaît.	
3 ... want to call back at 5 p.m.?	**a**	Je peux rappeler à 5 heures.	**3** ....
	b	Je parle à 5 heures.	
	c	Je veux téléphoner à 5 heures ?	
4 ... want to leave a message?	**a**	Un message, s'il vous plaît.	**4** ....
	b	C'est pour un message.	
	c	Je peux laisser un message ?	

Exercise 2

Claire is calling the agency. She wants to speak to Denis. Place the sentences in the right order to form a dialogue.

1 Un instant, je vous le passe. ....

2 Allô. Agence Charrain, bonjour. ....

3 C'est à quel sujet ? ....

4 Ça va, mais je ne peux pas venir à 8 heures. ....

5 Allô, ici Claire Dietz, je voudrais parler à Monsieur Moisson. ....

6 C'est pour un rendez-vous. ....

7 Ah c'est toi, bonjour Claire, ça va ? ....

8 Je peux venir à 9 heures ? ....

9 Pas de problème, rendez-vous à 9 heures. ....

Exercise 3

Review of numbers: Use a map of France to connect the numbers to the corresponding départements and place the answers in numerals in the middle row.

a zéro six .... Alpes-Maritimes

b treize .... Bouches-du-Rhône

c trente et un .... Haute Garonne

d trente-trois .... Gironde

e trente-quatre .... Hérault

f trente-huit .... Isère

g quarante-quatre .... Loire-Atlantique

h cinquante et un .... Marne

i cinquante-quatre .... Meurthe et Moselle

j soixante-sept .... Bas-Rhin

k soixante-neuf .... Rhône

l quatre-vingt-quatre .... Vaucluse

Exercise 4

Review of numbers: Use a map of France to connect the numbers to the corresponding départements and place the answers in numerals in the middle row.

1	Marseille	a	84	1	....
2	Lyon	b	69	2	....
3	Toulouse	c	67	3	....
4	Nancy	d	54	4	....
5	Nice	e	51	5	....
6	Avignon	f	44	6	....
7	Reims	g	38	7	....
8	Strasbourg	h	34	8	....
9	Grenoble	i	33	9	....
10	Bordeaux	j	31	10	....
11	Montpellier	k	131	11	....
12	Nantes	l	06	12	....

Exercise 5

Form the future tense of the verbs.

1 Elle (chercher) .... du travail à Paris.

2 Nous (donner) .... notre adresse à Claire.

3 Vous (parler) .... demain à Monsieur Charrain.

4 Tu (aimer) .... ce film.

5 Je (téléphoner) .... la semaine prochaine.

Exercise 6

Rewrite the sentences in the future tense.

1 Je ne suis pas là demain (tomorrow).

....

2 Madame Dietz téléphone à 8 heures.

....

3 Vous lui laissez un message.

....

4 J'ai le temps de la rencontrer la semaine prochaine (next week).

....

5 Je vais à Lyon vendredi. Nous allons voir un client.

....

Exercise 7

Translate:

I cannot interrupt Mr. Charrain. He is in a meeting. Leave your phone number, please. He will call you back at 6 o'clock.

....

....

....

....

....

....

Exercise 8

One word in each line is out of place. Which one?

1 le directeur	le client	la secrétaire
2 déranger	téléphoner	rappeler
3 la rencontre	le rendez-vous	la société
4 le numéro	la ligne	le voyage d'affaires

1 .... 2 .... 3 .... 4 ....

Vocabulary

Below is a list of vocabulary encoutered in this chapter.

agence de communication f	advertising agency	numéro de téléphone m	telephone number
C'est à quel sujet ?	About what?	parler à	to talk with/to
c'est exact	that's correct	poser sa candidature	to apply for (a job)
C.V. (cévé) m	CV (Curriculum Vitae)		
condition f	condition, term	professionnel	professional
court	short	raconter	to tell recount
déranger	to interrupt, disturb	rappeler	to call back (on the phone)
directeur m	director, manager	rencontrer	to get to know
discuter de	to discuss	réunion f	meeting
expérience f	experience	rien de prévu	nothing planned
je voudrais	I would like	stage m	internship
laisser	to leave	stagiaire m f	trainee intern
message m	message	Vous êtes libre ?	Are you free?

Test 3

Work your way around the board. Each correct answer will take you to the next question until you have completed the exercise. Enjoy!

1

Choose one of the two answers, then go to the square with the number of your answer.

2

Un billet ... Lille, s.v.p.!
pour   ▶ 8
à   ▶ 15

3

Wrong!

Go back to number 5.

8

Correct! Continue:
... allez-vous?
Quand   ▶ 6
Comment ▶ 25

9

Wrong!

Go back to number 25.

10

Wrong!

Go back to number 14.

11

Wrong!

Go back to number 29.

16

Good! Continue:
Le train ... parti.
est ▶ 22
a   ▶ 18

17

Wrong!

Go back to number 22.

18

Wrong!

Go back to number 16.

19

Correct!

End of exercise

24

Wrong!

Go back to number 12.

25

Very good! Continue:
Je travaille ... 8 jours.
depuis ▶ 14
pour   ▶ 9

26

Wrong!

Go back to number 30.

27

Good! Continue:
Vous ... où?
partent ▶ 23
partez   ▶ 12

4
Good! Continue:
Où est ... billet?
mon   ▶ 20
ma   ▶ 7

5
Correct! Continue:
Le train part ... 5 h.
pour   ▶ 3
à   ▶ 13

6
Wrong!

Go back to number 8.

7
Wrong!

Go back to number 4.

12
Very good!
Continue:
Vous arrivez quand?
le 2 avril   ▶ 16
2 avril   ▶ 24

13
Right! Continue:
On part au mois ... juin.
du   ▶ 21
de   ▶ 29

14
Very good! Continue:
Il ... à Lyon mardi.
iras   ▶ 10
ira   ▶ 30

15
Wrong!

Go back to number 2.

20
Well done! Continue:
Il fume moins ... moi.
que   ▶ 5
comme   ▶ 28

21
Wrong!

Go back to number 13.

22
Right!
Voilà ... adresse!
ma   ▶ 17
mon   ▶ 19

23
Wrong!

Go back to number 27.

28
Wrong!

Go back to number 20.

29
Great! Continue:
J'ai réservé du 2 ...
4 mai.
au   ▶ 27
à   ▶ 11

30
Right! Continue:
Le car s'arrête ... la
gare.
devant   ▶ 4
avant   ▶ 26

day:16

Work experience

Day 16 talks about preparing to find work experience. You will
also learn how to congugate the verb *mettre* and how to use the
incredibly useful *tout*. You will also further build your vocabulary
learning vocabulary that will help you to apply for work and fill in
official documentation. As usual, you will be able to practise what
you have learned with the exercises.

BUREAUCRACY...

*France loves bureaucracy and you will find there are offices to visit, queues to
be joined and forms to fill in for pretty much everything. While this can prove
testing for many the beginner learner, on the plus side, you are likely to meet
with just one person who will be dealing with your case from start to finish,
and you might even get to know them on a first-name basis!*

French conversation: CV pour le stage

Claire:	J'ai rendez-vous demain à l'agence. Je dois faire un C.V. en français. Vous pourriez corriger ce que j'ai préparé ?
Caroline:	Bien sûr, montre-moi ce que tu as fait.

Caroline lit le C.V.

Caroline:	Pour l'ordinateur: indique avec quels programmes tu as déjà travaillé. Tu pourrais préciser que tu as fait un bac, série économie, et dire en plus où tu as fait ta formation de secrétaire.
Claire:	Je ne sais pas si je dois mettre tous les stages que j'ai faits avant de commencer à travailler.
Caroline:	Il faut que tu mentionnes tous les stages où tu as fait un travail de secrétariat.
Claire:	Mon certificat de travail est en anglais. Je dois le joindre quand même à mon C.V. ?
Caroline:	Ça fait partie d'un dossier de candidature.
Claire:	Je dois rendre un C.V. écrit à la main ?
Caroline:	Non, tu peux le taper sur ordinateur, c'est plus lisible !

English conversation: CV for the internship

Claire:	I have an appointment at the agency tomorrow. I have to write a CV in French. Could you correct what I have prepared?
Caroline:	Sure, show me what you have written.

Caroline reads the CV.

Caroline:	As for as the computer: You should specify which programmes you have worked with already. You could also point out that you have the university entrance certificate in economics and state where you did your training as a secretary.
Claire:	I don't know whether I should list all the internships I did before I started work.
Caroline:	You must list all internships that had anything to do with secretarial work.
Claire:	My reference from work is in English. Should I attach it to the CV as well?
Caroline:	That is part of your application.
Claire:	Do I have to hand in a hand-written CV?
Caroline:	No, you can type it on the computer, that's more legible!

Grammar

Tout

tout le mois *(m)*	the whole month
toute la semaine *(f)*	the whole week
tout le voyage	the whole/entire journey
toute la ville	the whole city
tout un stage	a complete internship
toute une année	a whole year
tous les billets *(m pl)*	all tickets
toutes les places *(f pl)*	all places
tous ces touristes	all these tourists
tout mon argent	all my money

Tout (meaning all, everything) is a determiner that can accompany a noun. It must agree both in gender and number to that noun. Generally **tout** will precede another determiner (an article, demonstrative or possessive pronouns) in which case it is combined with **le/la/les** or **un/une/ce/mon**, etc.
In the singular form **tout/toute** means *whole, entire*, while the plural **tous**, **toutes** stands for *all*.

Quel

Quel meaning which should agree in gender and number with the noun to which it relates.

singular	plural
masculine	
quel	quels
Quel hôtel ?	Quels stages ?
Which hotel?	Which internships?
feminine	
Quelle agence ?	Quelles chambres ?
Which agency?	Which rooms?

Note:

Quelle heure est-il ?	What time is it?
Quel âge a-t-il/a-t-elle ?	How old is he/she?
J'ai réservé une chambre. Oui, à quel nom ?	I reserved a room. Yes, in whose name?

Verbs: Mettre (to put)

The verb **mettre** can have a variety of different meanings. It's principal meaning is to put, to place, to lay, to put on, as in **mettre les clés sur la table**, place the keys on the table.

When used relating to clothing **mettre** takes on the meaning of to dress, to put on, as in **mettre son manteau**.

In the example below, it takes on the meaning of 'listing':

Je dois mettre tous les stages ?	Must I list all the internships?

present tense:

je mets	nous mettons
tu mets	vous mettez
il/elle met	ils/elles mettent

perfect tense:

j'ai mis

Exercises

Exercise 1

Fill in the correct form of tout.

1 J'ai travaillé .... la journée (the whole day).

2 J'ai lu .... les dossiers de candidature.

3 J'ai téléphoné à . ... les candidats.

4 J'ai des rendez-vous .... le mois de mai.

Exercise 2

Follow the example below and ask questions with quel, quelle, quels or quelles.

Tu connais ce film ?   *Quel film ?*

1 Tu connais cette ville ? ....

2 Je fais un stage. ....

3 Tu as l'adresse *(f)* ? ....

4 Tu me donnes un journal ? ....

5 J'ai des problèmes *(m pl)*. ....

6 Je cherche les clés (keys, *f pl*)..

7 N'oublie pas ton rendez-vous ! ....

8 Tu as lu l'annonce *(f)* ? ....

Exercise 3

Fill in the present tense form.

1 Qu'est-ce tu (mettre) .... aujourd'hui ?

2 Je (mettre) .... une jupe et un pull.

3 Elle (mettre) .... les bagages dans la voiture.

4 Vous (mettre) .... une annonce dans le journal ?

5 Ils (mettre) .... les dossiers sur le bureau.

Exercise 4

Using the following example, insert tout, toute, tous or toutes.

.... les matins: jogging à 7 heures.   *Tous les matins: jogging à 7 heures.*

1 .... les après-midi: visites guidées de la région.

2 .... les soirs: cinéma et discothèque.

3 .... les semaines: invitations dans une famille française.

4 Notre club est ouvert .... l'année.

5 .... les étudiants et .... les étudiantes sont invités au club.

6 A la cafétéria, ... les repas sont service compris.

7 A l'Alliance française .... les professeurs ont le français comme langue maternelle.

8 Dans notre école les étudiants sont de .... les nationalités.

9 .... les stages d'informatique sont en anglais.

10 Elle a fait .... son travail en quatre heures.

11 L'agence répond à .... les candidatures.

12 Mentionnez .... les langues que vous parlez.

Exercise 5

Translate the following passage into French.

I have a meeting at 9 a.m. tomorrow morning at the agency. I have to write a CV in French. I'm writing it on the computer, that's easier to read. I have done plenty of internships abroad (à l'étranger).

....

....

....

....

....

....

Vocabulary

Below is a list of vocabulary encountered in this chapter.

à la place de	instead of	montrer à	to show to
avant de	before	ordinateur m	computer
bac m	university entrance certificate	oublier	to forget
		parlé et écrit	written and spoken
bac série économie	university entrance cert. in economics	préciser	to mention
bonne maîtrise de …	very good knowledge of …	programme m	program(me)
		quand même	as well
ce que	what (relative pronoun)	rendre	to hand in
célibataire	single (not married)	si	if/whether/in case
certificat de travail m	work cert	taper sur l'ordinateur	to write on the computer
commencer (à + infinitive)	to start (doing something)	tous	all
		tu pourrais (pouvoir)	you could (informal)
corriger	to correct	vous pourriez (pouvoir)	you could (formal)
courant	fluent(ly)	divorce m	divorce
déjà	already	divorcé(e)	divorced
dire	to say	état civil m	marital status
écrit à la main	handwritten	études f pl	studies
en français	in French	femme f	woman, wife
faire partie de	to be a part of	mari m	husband
demain	tomorrow	mariage m	marriage
il faut que tu …	you must	marié(e)	married
je mettrais	I would write	nationalité f	nationality
joindre	to add, attach, enclose	né(e)	née (born)
langue maternelle m	mother tongue	situation de famille f	marital status
lisible	legible	veuf, veuve	widower/widow
mentionner	to mention		
mettre	to list, specify; to put		

The internship

Day 17 delves further into the future tense (check back to Day 15 for more on this). You will continue to build your vocabulary and learn more about the work etiquette in France. Finally, you will be able to check your progress using the exercises in this chapter.

WORK ETIQUETTE...

*Young people at work generally address each other with the more familiar **tu** if they are all roughly of the same age and status.*

*Superiors generally address their secretary (or personal assistant) with **vous** and their first name. You should always address your boss and senior management with **vous**.*

French conversation: Premier jour à l'agence

Secrétaire:	Bonjour, Mademoiselle. Suivez-moi, je vais vous montrer votre bureau et vous présenter ... Denis, je vous présente notre nouvelle stagiaire. Denis vous parlera en détail de l'organisation de notre agence. Voilà, je vous laisse. Si vous avez des questions, je suis à votre disposition.
Denis:	Félicitations pour le stage! Notre agence est petite mais très dynamique. Nous avons des clients dans toute l'Europe. La moyenne d'âge est jeune, l'ambiance décontractée, tout le monde se tutoie ici.
Claire:	Alors je vais en faire autant. Dis-moi, qu'est-ce que j'aurai à faire ?
Denis:	Tu seras mon assistante. Nous organiserons ensemble les voyages d'affaires, les rencontres professionnelles avec nos clients étrangers.
Claire:	Montre-moi le calendrier des prochaines rencontres !
Denis:	On ira à Cannes au mois de juin pour le festival international du Film Publicitaire. Pour nous, c'est l'événement le plus important de l'année !
Claire:	Super ! Ce sera la première fois que j'irai sur la Côte !

English conversation: First day at the agency

Secretary:	Good morning! Come with me, I'll show you your office and introduce you ... Denis, here's our new intern. Denis will speak to you in detail about the structure of our agency. OK, I'll leave you two. If you have any questions, I'll be available.
Denis:	Congratulations on your internship! Our agency is small but very dynamic. We have clients all over Europe. The average age of the people working here is young, we have a relaxed atmosphere and everyone says 'tu' to each other.
Claire:	I'll do the same then. Tell me, what do I have to do?
Denis:	You'll be my assistant. Together we will organize business trips and business meetings with our foreign clients.
Claire:	Show me the next meetings diaried in the desk calendar.
Denis:	In June we'll go to Cannes to attend the International Festival of Advertising. That is the most important event of the year for us!
Claire:	Great! That'll be the first I've been to the Côte d'Azur!

Grammar

Future tense with aller + infinitive

There are two ways to form the future in French, the **futur simple** (see also Day 15) and the **futur proche**.

The **futur simple** as in **j'irai à Londres l'année prochaine** (I will go to London next year), is used to express a firm intention, while the exact time of the action is not yet clear.

The **futur proche** (immediate future), as in **je vais faire un stage le mois prochain** (I'll be doing an internship next month) refers mostly to the imminent future. The French use of the **futur proche** with **aller** + infinitive corresponds closely to the English use of "going to". **Je vais montrer son bureau à Claire.**   I will show Claire her office

The **futur proche** is used to express an intention or an action that will take place in the immediate future. The **futur proche** is formed by combining the **present tense** of **aller** (to go) and the infinitive of the verb.

Je vais téléphoner dans une heure	I will call in an hour.
Tu vas téléphoner à Florent ?	Are you going to call Florent?
Il/elle/on va téléphoner à Cannes.	He/she is going to call Cannes.
Nous allons téléphoner à 8 heures.	We'll call at 8p.m.
Vous allez téléphoner à Londres ?	Are you going to call London?
Ils/elles vont téléphoner à l'agence.	They are going to call the agency.

The negative forms **ne ... pas** (not), **ne ... plus** (no more, not any more) etc. should be placed on either side of the conjugated verb form of **aller** as shown in the examples below:

Je *ne* vais *pas* téléphoner.	I will not phone.
Tu *ne* vas *plus* téléphoner à Florent.	You will not phone Florent any more.
Il *ne* va *pas* réparer la voiture.	He will not repair the car.

Exercises

Exercise 1

Using the following example, put the sentences into the **futur proche**.

J'ai travaillé dans une agence. Je (travailler) *Je vais travailler dans une agence.*

1 Il a été directeur. Il (être)

....

2 Elle a organisé la réunion. Elle (organiser)

....

3 J'ai mangé un steak au poivre. Je (manger)

....

4 Denis a invité Claire. Denis (inviter)

....

5 Nous avons fait du ski. Nous (faire du ski)

....

6 J'ai acheté les billets. Je (acheter)

....

7 Le car pour Chamrousse est parti. Le car pour Chamrousse (partir)

....

8 On a pris un forfait. On (prendre)

....

Exercise 2

Insert the **futur simple** (see Day 15).

1 Denis (parler) .... de l'organisation de l'agence.

2 Il (montrer) .... son bureau à Claire.

3 Claire (avoir) .... un collègue sympathique.

4 Denis (être) .... souvent en voyage d'affaires.

5 Ils (aller) .... ensemble à Cannes.

6 Ils (rencontrer) .... des clients.

7 Claire (aller) .... pour la première fois sur la Côte.

8 Denis et Claire (prendre) .... le train pour aller à Cannes.

Exercise 3

Translate teh following text into French:

I work in an advertising agency. The agency is small, but dynamic. The average age is young, the atmosphere is relaxed. We have clients all over Europe. In June we will go to Cannes.

....

....

....

....

....

....

Exercise 4

One word in each line is out of place. Which one?

1	jeune	dynamique	facile	faire
2	affaires	questions	clients	son
3	sommes	serons	serai	seras
4	auront	aurai	aurez	avez
5	irons	allons	irai	ira

1 .... **2** .... **3** .... **4** .... **5** ....

Vocabulary

Below is a list of vocabulary encountered in this chapter.

affaires *f pl*	*business*	**premier**	*first*
ambiance *f*	*atmosphere/mood*	**ici**	*here*
assistante *f*	*assistant f*	**important**	*important; significant*
autant	*as much, as well, like*	**jeune**	*young*
avoir à faire	*to have to do*	**laisser**	*to leave*
bureau *m*	*office*	**moyenne d'âge** *f*	*average age*
calendrier *m*	*desk calendar, schedule*	**nouvel**	*new*
client *m*	*client, customer*	**organisation** *f*	*structure, organization*
décontracté	*relaxed*	**organiser**	*to organize*
dynamique	*dynamic*	**prochain**	*next*
en détail	*in detail*	**professionnel**	*professional*
ensemble	*together*	**rencontre**	*business meeting*
étranger	*foreign*	**professionnelle** *f*	
étranger *m*	*abroad*	**publicitaire**	*advertisement*
être à la	*to be available*	**publicité** *f*	*advertising*
disposition de		**question** *f*	*question*
événement *m*	*event*	**suivre (suivez)**	*to join, follow*
Félicitations ! *f pl*	*Congratulations!*	**tout le monde**	*all, everybody*
festival du film	*advertising film festival*	**très**	*very*
publicitaire		**voyage**	*business trip*
film *m*	*film, movie*	**d'affaires** *m*	
fois *f*	*times*		

Going out

Day 18 covers the imperfect tense of *être* (to be) and verbs ending in *-er*. You will also learn how to improve your conversation skills and learn how to make plans and suggestions. You will also learn about Parisian nightlife.

A NIGHT OUT IN PARIS...

*Two indispensable magazines for Parisian nightlife are **Pariscope** and **l'Officiel des spectacles**. They contain everything there is to know about the cultural life of the city, including what's on in the theatre and cinema, concerts and exhibitions, and a directory of cafés and restaurants. Listings include addresses, opening times and the nearest **Métro**.*

French conversation: Soirée collègues

Denis:	Dis donc, si on allait à un concert samedi prochain ?
Claire:	Oui, quel concert ?
Denis:	Tu connais Patricia Kaas? Elle passe au »Zénith«.
Claire:	Super! Il paraît qu'elle est géniale sur scène. Elle a une voix extraordinaire.
Denis:	Il faut acheter les billets à l'avance.
Claire:	Moi, j'ai le temps d'y aller demain. Tu as une idée du prix des places ?
Denis:	Entre €18 et €50 je pense.

Au »Zénith«. A la fin du concert, applaudissements, un spectateur (Abel) s'approche de Claire.

Abel:	Ça vous a plu ?
Claire:	Oui, beaucoup, et vous ?
Abel:	C'était génial! Excusez-moi, mais on ne vous a jamais dit que vous ressemblez un peu à Patricia Kaas ? Vous avez la même coupe de cheveux, et le même regard qu'elle.
Claire:	Vous exagérez! C'est la première fois qu'on me dit ça !
Abel:	En plus, vous avez l'accent belge !
Claire:	Non, non, vous vous trompez ! Je suis anglaise et vous, vous êtes algérien ?
Abel:	Non, je suis français enfin ... beur, si vous préférez. On pourrait prendre un pot ensemble ?
Claire:	Désolée, je suis avec des amis. On finit la soirée aux »Bains«. Viens avec nous, si tu veux !
Abel:	Ben, ouais, pourquoi pas ! Ça t'ennuie si je te tutoie aussi ?
Claire:	Pas du tout !

English conversation: An evening out with colleagues

Denis:	Say, how about going to a concert together next Saturday?
Claire:	Yes! What kind of concert?
Denis:	Do you know Patricia Kaas? She's playing at the "Zénith".
Claire:	Great! They say she is really good live. She has a great voice.
Denis:	We have to buy the tickets in advance.
Claire:	I have time tomorrow to get them. Do you have any idea how much the tickets cost?
Denis:	Between €18 and €50, I think.

At the "Zénith". At the end of the concert, applause, a spectator (Abel) approaches Claire.

Abel:	Did you like it?
Claire:	Yes, very much so, did you?
Abel:	It was great! Excuse me, but has anybody ever told you that you look a little like Patricia Kaas? You have the same haircut and the same look.
Claire:	You're exaggerating! That's the first time anyone has said that to me.
Abel:	What's more you have a Belgian accent.
Claire:	Oh no, you're mistaken! I'm English, and what about you, are you Algerian?
Abel:	No I'm French, well ... beur*, if you prefer. Would you like to have a drink with me?
Claire:	Sorry, I'm here with some friends. We're going to the nightclub "Bains" afterwards. You can join us, if you want!
Abel:	Well, yeah, why not! Would you mind if I used 'tu'?
Claire:	Not at all.

* descendants of the Immigrants from the Mahgreb states in northern Africa are sometimes called beur

Grammar

The imperfect tense of *être* and verbs ending in *-er*

C'était génial !	That was great!
Elle cherchait du travail.	She was looking for work.

To form the imperfect tense (**imparfait**) the following endings are added to the stem of the 1st person plural of the verb's present tense: **-ais, -ais, -ait, -ions, -iez, -aient**.

Imperfect tense of verbs ending in *-er*

chercher (to search/look for)	
je cherchais	nous cherchions
tu cherchais	vous cherchiez
il/elle on cherchait	ils/elles cherchaient

être	
j'étais (I was)	nous étions
tu étais	vous étiez
il/elle/on était	ils/elles étaient

The **imparfait** (imperfect) is used to indicate something that was continuing, uncompleted or interrupted by another event. It is also used to describe a customary habit or recurring events in the past.

Making suggestions

Si on allait au cinéma ?
How about going/Shall we go to the cinema?
On pourrait aller au cinéma !
We could go to the cinema!

To make a suggestion you could use **si** + **imparfait** as in: *Si on allait* au cinéma ? or use the conditional (see Day 26) + infinitive: *On pourrait aller* au cinéma !

Verbs: dire (to say)

present tense	
je dis	nous disons
tu dis	vous dites
il/elle dit	ils/elles disent

future tense	
je dirais	nous dirons
tu diras	vous direz
il/elle dira	ils/elles diront

perfect tense	
j'ai dit	tu as dit etc

imperfect tense	
je disais	nous disions
tu disais	vous disiez
il/elle disait	ils/elles disaient

Exercises

Exercise 1

Fill in the imperfect tense of the verbs.

1 En 1985 je (être) .... à Rome.

2 Il (arriver) .... toujours (always) à huit heures.

3 Nous (inviter) .... souvent (often) Claire au restaurant.

4 Vous (parler) .... souvent de vos voyages à l'étranger.

5 Tu (téléphoner) .... tous les jours à Michel.

6 La secrétaire (être) .... malade hier (yesterday).

7 On (accompagner) .... toujours Julie à la maternelle.

8 Je (aimer) .... faire du ski.

Exercise 2

Make suggestions as in the following example.

Si on (aller) au cinéma ?   *Si on allait au cinéma ?*

1 Si on (partir) en vacances en Espagne ?

....

2 Si on (prendre) le TGV pour Lyon ?

....

3 Si on (faire) des crêpes ?

....

4 Si on (téléphoner) à Abel ?

....

5 Si on (louer) une voiture ?

....

6 Si on (acheter) le Figaro ?

....

7 Si on (inviter) Claire dimanche ?

....

8 Si on (discuter) de ta candidature ?

....

Exercise 3

Fill in the present tense forms of dire.

Abel (dire) .... que Claire ressemble à Patricia Kaas. Les amis de Claire (dire) ....

qu'ils vont finir la soirée dans une disco. Qu'est-ce que vous (dire) .... ? Je (dire) ....

que c'est la première fois que je vais à un concert au Zénith.

Exercise 4

Join up the questions with the correct answers.

1 Vous êtes belge ?	**a** C'était génial !
2 Ça vous a plu ?	**b** Non, je suis anglaise.
3 On pourrait prendre un pot ?	**c** Vous exagérez !
4 Vous ressemblez à amis.	**d** Désolée, je suis avec des Patricia Kaas !

1 .... 2 .... 3 .... 4 ....

Exercsie 5

Put the sentences in the right order.

1 Claire est allée au concert avec Denis. ....

2 Elle a rencontré Abel à la fin du concert. ....

3 Samedi, Patricia Kaas passait au Zénith. ....

4 Abel a demandé à Claire si elle était belge. ....

5 Claire, Denis et Abel sont allés tous les trois aux »Bains« après le concert. ....

6 Claire a dit qu'elle était anglaise. ....

7 Le concert a beaucoup plu à Claire et à Abel. ....

8 JAbel a dit à Claire qu'elle ressemblait un peu à Patricia Kaas. ....

9 C'est Claire qui a acheté les billets de concert. ....

10 Denis a proposé (suggest) à Claire d'aller à ce concert. ....

Exercise 6

Who's who? Form a sentence by establishing the connection between the words in each line as in the following example.

John Kennedy/Etats-Unis/président   *John Kennedy, c'était un président américain*

1 John Lennon/Angleterre/musicien

....

2 Leonardo da Vinci/Italie/peintre

....

3 Greta Garbo/Suède/actrice

....

4 Einstein/Allemagne/physicien

....

5 Hiro-Hito/Japon/empereur

....

6 Jean Gabin/France/acteur

....

7 Agatha Christie/Angleterre/romancière

....

8 Vasco da Gama/Portugal/navigateur

....

Exercise 7

One word in each line is out of place. Which one?

1	super	génial	oui	extraordinaire
2	concert	plu	scène	billet
3	désolé	belge	beur	étranger
4	demain	aujourd'hui	hier	si
5	tu	moi	mois	te

1 .... **2** .... **3** .... **4** .... **5** ....

Vocabulary

Below is a list of vocabulary encountered in this chapter.

à l'avance	*in advance*	**génial**	*great*
accent *m*	*accent*	**hier**	*yesterday*
acheter	*to buy*	**le Zénith**	*Parisian concert venue*
algérien	*Algerian*	**même**	*(the) same*
avoir une	*to have an idea*	**pas du tout**	*not at all*
idée de		**passer**	*to appear on stage*
belge	*Belgian*	**plu (plaire)**	*to enjoy, like*
ben, ouais	*well yeah*	**pourquoi pas**	*why not*
billet *m*	*ticket*	**prendre un pot**	*to have a drink*
ça t'ennuie	*would you mind if . . .*	**regard** *m*	*look, view*
(ennuyer) si . . .		**ressembler à**	*to have in common, look*
collègue *m/f*	*colleague*		*like*
concert *m*	*concert*	**s'approcher de**	*to approach someone*
coupe de	*haircut*	**se tromper**	*to be mistaken*
cheveux		**spectateur** *m*	*spectator*
dit (dire)	*said*	**super**	*super*
ensemble	*together*	**toujours**	*always*
entre	*between*	**tutoyer (tutoie)**	*to address with the formal*
exagérer	*exaggerate*		**'tu'**
extraordinaire	*great, extraordinairy*	**un peu**	*a little*
fin *f*	*end*	**voix** *f*	*voice*
soirée *f*	*evening*		

Celebrations

Day 19 covers verbs ending in *-ir* and you will learn how to conjugate the verbs *offrir* (to offer), *ouvrir* (to open) and *voir* (to see). You will also learn lots more useful vocabulary, from this chapter and more, and you will pick up some more cultural tips.

INVITATIONS...

When you are invited to someone's home in France, it is appropriate to bring a gift for the host. Flowers and wine are a popular choice. If buying flowers, make sure that the presentation is as beautiful as the flowers themselves - these details do matter in France. Avoid offering chrysanthemums as these are traditionally used at funerals.

If you're invited at a set time for an **apéritif**, *never show up exactly on time. You are expected to give the host a little extra time to prepare so you should aim to arrive about 15 minutes after the agreed time.*

French conversation: Qu'est-ce qu'on fait ce soir ?

Chez Denis. C'est son anniversaire. Claire et Miko lui ont apporté des fleurs et un cadeau.

Claire:	Joyeux anniversaire, Denis !
Miko:	Bon anniversaire, tiens, c'est pour toi !
Denis:	N'oubliez pas, d'abord la bise et après le cadeau ! C'est la première fois qu'on m'offre d'aussi belles fleurs, des tulipes rouges, j'adore! Et ça, qu'est-ce que c'est ?
Miko:	Ouvre, tu verras bien! Si tu l'as déjà, on peut l'échanger.
Denis:	Le dernier disque compact de Véronique Sanson, j'ai failli me l'acheter hier. Génial !
Claire:	On voulait t'inviter dans un resto japonais. Ça te va ?
Denis:	On va commencer par un verre de champagne pour fêter mon anniversaire. J'avais pensé vous emmener aux »Bouffes du Nord«, c'est superbe comme théâtre, je m'y suis pris trop tard, ce soir, c'est complet.
Miko:	Ce sera pour une autre fois! Ça ne te dit rien, le resto japonais ?
Denis:	Si, je veux bien. Mais après le resto, on pourrait aller retrouver mes copains dans un club de jazz, »le New Morning«.
Claire:	Et si on allait danser dans une boîte africaine ?
Denis:	La nuit sera longue. On peut toujours commencer par »le New Morning« et après on verra.
Miko:	Je vois que c'est la grande forme !
Denis:	On n'a pas 25 ans tous les jours ! Allons-y ! Mais c'est moi qui vous invite au resto !

English conversation: What shall we do tonight?

At Denis' place. It is his birthday. Claire and Miko brought him flowers and a present.

Claire: Happy birthday, Denis!
Miko: All the best on your birthday, here, this is for you!
Denis: Don't forget, first the kiss and then the present! That's the first time I've been given such wonderful flowers; I love red tulips! And what's that?
Miko: Open it, you'll see! If you have it already we can exchange it.
Denis: The latest CD from Véronique Sanson, I almost bought it myself yesterday. Great!
Claire: We wanted to invite you to a Japanese restaurant. What do you think?
Denis: Let's start celebrating my birthday with a glass of champagne. I had thought of inviting you to the "Bouffes du Nord", which is a wonderful theatre, but I was too late and it was sold out for tonight.
Miko: Leave that for another time. And the Japanese restaurant doesn't tempt you in any way?
Denis: It certainly does. But after the restaurant we could meet my friends in a jazz club, the "New Morning".
Claire: How about going dancing in an African nightclub?
Denis: This will be a long night. We can start at the "New Morning" and then we'll see.
Claire: I see you are in great shape today!
Denis: You don't turn 25 every day! Let's go! But it's my treat!

Grammar

Verbs ending in -ir: offrir (to give), ouvrir (to open), voir (to see)

present tense		
j'offre	j'ouvre	je vois
tu offres	tu ouvres	tu vois
il/elle offre	il/elle ouvre	il/elle voit
nous offrons	nous ouvrons	nous voyons
vous offrez	vous ouvrez	vous voyez
ils/elles offrent	ils/elles ouvrent	ils/elles voient

perfect tense:		
j'ai offert	j'ai ouvert	j'ai vu

future tense:		
j'offrirai	j'ouvrirai	je verrai
tu offriras	tu ouvriras	tu verras
il/elle offrira	il/elle ouvrira	il/elle verra
nous offrirons	nous ouvrirons	nous verrons
vous offrirez	vous ouvrirez	vous verrez
ils/elles offriront	ils/elles ouvriront	ils/elles verront

imperfect tense:		
j'offrais	j'ouvrais	je voyais
tu offrais	tu ouvrais	tu voyais
il/elle offrait	il/elle ouvrait	il/elle voyait
nous offrions	nous ouvrions	nous voyions
vous offriez	vous ouvriez	vous voyiez
ils/elles offraient	ils/elles ouvraient	ils/elles voyaient

pour + infinitive: to (in order to)

On va chez Denis *pour fêter* son anniversaire.
We are going to Denis' **to celebrate** his birthday.
Je prends le train *pour aller* à Grenoble.
I am taking the train **to go** to Grenoble.

Exercises

Exercise 1

Fill in the present tense forms of the verbs.

Je (voir) .... la bouteille de Bourgueil, elle (être) .... sur la table. Il (ouvrir) ....
la bouteille avec un tire-bouchon (cork screw). Elles (offrir) .... un disque à Denis. Denis
(avoir) .... 25 ans. Ils (vouloir) .... aller écouter du jazz dans un club.

Exercise 2

Using the following example, form sentences with pour +infinitive.

Elle part mardi. Elle va à Cannes.   *Elle part mardi pour aller à Cannes.*

1 Ils achètent des billets. Ils vont au concert.

....

2 On prend un verre de champagne. On fête l'anniversaire de Denis.

....

3 Elle téléphone au bureau. Elle prend rendez-vous.

....

4 Je fais un cours de français. Je vais travailler à Paris.

....

5 Vous faites un stage de ski. Vous apprenez (apprendre – to learn) à faire du ski.

....

6 Elles cherchent un hôtel. Elles restent trois jours à Londres.

....

7 Je vais aller à la poste. J'achète une télécarte.

....

8 On prend un kilo de tomates. On fait une salade.

....

Exercise 3

What do you say when you want to . . .

1 . . . congratulate someone on his/her
birthday

   a Bonne fête !

   b Bon anniversaire !

   c Félicitations !

2 . . . give someone a present?

   a Voilà !

   b Prends ça.

   c Tiens, c'est pour toi !

3 . . . say thanks for a present?

   a Merci pour les tulipes, c'est très gentil !

   b Je n'aime pas les tulipes !

   c Pourquoi des tulipes rouges ?

4 . . . invite someone for a meal?

   a Tu viens au restaurant ?

   b Je t'invite au restaurant !

   c Tu aimes les restaurants japonais ?

1 .... **2** .... **3** .... **4** ....

Exercise 4

Fill in the verbs in the future tense.

1 Pour son anniversaire Miko (inviter) .... ses copains chez elle.

2 Je lui (offrir) .... deux billets de concert.

3 Denis lui (offrir) .... des fleurs.

4 Elle (ouvrir) .... une bouteille de champagne.

5 Nous (commencer) .... la soirée à huit heures.

6 Après le champagne, on (manger) .... des spécialités japonaises.

7 A dix heures on (retrouver) .... des copains au New Morning.

8 La nuit (être) .... longue, on (rentrer) .... à cinq heures du matin.

Exercise 5

Make a dialogue by joining the sentences.

1 Allô Denis ? C'est Dominique.

2 Bien! Bon anniversaire !

3 A Paris, pour le weekend.

4 Rien de spécial !

5 D'accord, je prends un taxi !

6 Je n'ai pas de cadeau pour toi !

a Merci, tu es où ?

b Viens boire le champagne !

c Ah c'est toi, salut ! Ça va ?

d Qu'est-ce que tu fais ce soir ?

e Ça ne fait rien !

f On t'attend pour le champagne !

1 .... 2 .... 3 .... 4 .... 5 .... 6 ....

Exercise 6

Translate:

It's my birthday. Thank you very much for the Miles Davis CD. I invite you to the restaurant. Afterwards we could go dancing. This will be a long night!

....

....

....

....

....

....

Vocabulary

Below is a list of vocabulary encountered in this chapter.

allons-y	*let's go*	**fleur** *f*	*flower*
anniversaire *m*	*birthday*	**j'ai failli**	*I almost*
apporter	*to bring (along)*	**Joyeux**	*Happy*
après	*after/afterwards*	**anniversaire!**	*birthday!*
avoir 25 ans	*to turn 25(years old)*	**nuit** *f*	*night*
bise *f*	*kiss*	**offrir**	*to give*
boîte *f*	*nightclub*	**on voulait**	*we wanted*
bon anniversaire	*Happy birthday*	**(vouloir)**	
C'est la forme!	*You are in shape/on form*	**oublier**	*to forget*
ça me dit	*that sounds good to me*	**ouvrir**	*to open (up)*
cadeau *m*	*gift*	**penser**	*to think*
complet	*sold out; full; complete*	**retrouver**	*to meet*
copain *m*	*friend*	**s'y prendre**	*taking care of something*
disque	*CD*	**trop tard**	*far too late*
compact *m*		**théâtre** *m*	*theatre*
échanger	*to exchange*	**Tiens ! (tenir)**	*Take (it)!*
emmener	*to take along, to bring*	**tous les jours**	*every day*
fêter	*to celebrate*	**tulipe** *f*	*tulip*

day:20

Driving in France

Day 20 covers how to use the pronoun *lequel* (meaning which one?). You will also learn how to use the conditional tense to suggest you may do something. Finally, you will also discover some important country information about renting a car and driving in France.

RULES OF THE ROAD...

When driving in France, it is important to remember that on main roads, traffic on the major road has priority. This may seem like common sense but on smaller roads with no signposts, it may cause confusion. If in doubt, always remember to give **priorité à droite** *(give way to the right). If an oncoming driver flashes their headlights, it is to indicate that he or she has priority, not that you should go first! A* **yellow diamond sign** *indicates that you have priority; a* **diamond sign with a diagonal black line** *indicates you do not.*

French conversation: Location de voiture

Employée:	Qu'est-ce que je peux faire pour vous ?
Denis:	Nous voulons nous renseigner sur le prix d'une voiture de location.
Employée:	Qu'est-ce que vous voulez comme voiture ?
Claire:	Une petite voiture qui ne consomme pas beaucoup d'essence.
Employée:	Alors je vous propose une Clio ou une Golf. Elles coûtent toutes les deux s100 par jour. Laquelle préférez-vous ? Pour une semaine vous avez un forfait de €320 avec kilométrage illimité.
Denis:	Le forfait pour une semaine est intéressant, mais nous partons seulement trois jours pour le week-end de Pâques.
Employée:	Dans ce cas, je peux vous faire aussi un forfait pour trois jours, €200 toutes taxes comprises (T.T.C.) si vous ramenez la voiture ici. Si vous la laissez dans une autre agence, il y a un supplément de €25.
Denis:	Alors on va prendre la Clio du vendredi soir au lundi.
Employée:	D'accord, je vous prépare le contrat. J'ai besoin du permis de conduire du conducteur. Pensez à faire le plein avant de rendre la voiture. Vous désirez régler la caution en espèces ou avec une carte de crédit ?
Denis:	En espèces.

English conversation: Car rental

Employee:	What can I do for you?
Denis:	We'd like to inquire about prices for a rental car.
Employee:	What kind of car do you want?
Claire:	A small car with low petrol/gas consumption.
Employee:	Then I'd suggest a Clio or a Golf. Both are €100 per day. Which one do you prefer? You get a flat rate of €320 for a week with unlimited mileage.
Denis:	The flat rate for one week is interesting, but we're only going away for three days over the Easter weekend.
Employee:	In that case I can also offer you a flat rate for three days, €200, all-inclusive, if you return the car here. If you return it at another branch there's a surcharge of €25.
Denis:	We'll take the Clio then, from Friday evening until Monday.
Employee:	OK, I'll prepare the contract. I need the driver's driving licence. Remember to fill the tank before you return the car. Would you like to pay the deposit in cash or with your credit card?
Denis:	In cash.

Grammar

The interrogative pronoun *lequel*

Lequel is an interrogative pronoun, which takes the gender and number of the noun it relates to.
Lequel/laquelle/lesquels/lesquelles can refer to people as well as objects.

	singular	plural
masculine	lequel	lesquels
feminine	laquelle	lesquelles

Nous voulons louer *une voiture. Laquelle préférez-vous ?*
Which one would you prefer?

avant de + the infinitive: (before)

singular	plural

J'ai fait le plein *avant de rendre* la voiture.
I filled the tank, **before** I returned the car.

In this construction the main sentence and the part of the sentence with the infinitive must share the same subject.

Conditional si

The conditional **si** (meaning *if*) **never** takes the future tense. Only the main clause that follows can take the present or future tense.

Si vous prenez la voiture une semaine, c'est moins cher.
If you hire the car for a week, it will be cheaper.

S'il vient à Paris, on ira au concert.
If he comes to Paris, he will go to the concert.

Note:
si + **il/ils** becomes **s'il/s'ils**. With **elle/elles** it remains the same: **si elle(s)...**

Exercises

Exercise 1

Using the following example, fill in the correct form of lequel.

Voilà deux pulls. *Lequel préférez-vous ?* (Here are two sweaters. Which one do you prefer?)

1 Voilà deux bières. .... préférez-vous ?

2 Voilà deux fromages. .... préférez-vous ?

3 Voilà deux chambres. .... préférez-vous ?

4 Voilà deux hôtels. .... préférez-vous ?

5 Voilà deux tartes. .... préférez-vous ?

Exercise 2

Using the following example, form a sentence with avant de.

Nous partons. Nous téléphonons à Caroline.

Nous téléphonons à Caroline avant de partir.

1 Nous louons une voiture. Nous demandons le prix.

....

2 Nous partons en week-end. Nous réservons une chambre.

....

3 Elle téléphone à Cannes. Elle organise le voyage d'affaires.

....

4 Ils vont au concert. Ils achètent les billets.

....

5 Elles vont chez Luis. Elles achètent des fleurs.

....

Exercice 3

Using the following example, form a sentence with si.

Vous prenez la voiture une semaine. C'est moins cher.

Si vous prenez la voiture une semaine, c'est moins cher.

1 Vous allez en voiture (by car) à Tours. C'est moins cher.

....

2 Vous visitez le Louvre en semaine (during the week). C'est plus intéressant.

....

3 Tu téléphones à Claire à 8 heures. Elle sera là.

....

4 Tu rentres à 7 heures. On ira au cinéma.

....

5 Nous partons faire du ski. Nous réserverons deux chambres.

....

Exercice 4

Make a dialogue by joining the sentences.

1 Qu'est-ce que je peux faire pour vous ?   **a** Pour trois jours seulement.

2 Qu'est-ce que vous voulez comme voiture ?   **b** Nous désirons louer une petite voiture.

3 Vous la prenez pour combien de temps ?   **c** Avec une carte de crédit.

4 Vous voulez un forfait ?   **d** Une Clio.

5 Vous désirez régler comment ?   **e** D'accord, mais un forfait pour trois jours.

1 ....   **2** ....   **3** ....   **4** ....   **5** ....

Exercise 5

Ask questions using quel (as in Day 16).

1 .... est ton adresse ?

2 .... est ton numéro de téléphone ?

3 .... est ta langue maternelle ?

4 .... est ta nationalité ?

5 On a rendez-vous à . ... heure au café ?

6 Toi aussi, tu vas au concert, ... jour ?

7 .... âge a Claire ?

8 Tu travailles pour .... agences à Paris ?

9 Tu lis .... journal ?

10 Tu parles couramment .... langues ?

11 Tu as .... professeur ?

12 Tu fais du sport? .... sports ?

Exercise 6

Using the following example, form comparative sentences.

Clio/Golf/chère   *Une Clio est plus chère qu'une Golf.*

1 forfait pour 1 semaine/prix à la journée/intéressant

....

2 billets de cinéma/billets de concert/chers

....

3 le japonais/l'anglais/difficile

....

4 la France/l'Italie/grande

....

5 vacances scolaires/en France en Allemagne/longues

....

6 fromages français/fromages allemands/plus connus

....

7 TGV/train normal/rapide (fast)

....

8 hôtels en province/hôtels à Paris/chers

....

Vocabulary

Below is a list of vocabulary encountered in this chapter.

alors	then	**louer**	to rent
autre	other	**Pâques** m	Easter
avoir besoin de	to need	**permis de**	driving licence
carte de crédit f	credit card	**conduire** m	
caution f	deposit	**petit**	small
conducteur m	(car) driver	**préparer**	to prepare
consommer	to consume	**proposer**	to suggest
contrat m	contract	**ramener**	to return
coûter	to cost	**régler**	to pay
dans ce cas	in that case	**rendre**	to return
en espèces	in cash	**sans plomb**	lead free/unleaded
essence f	petrol/gas	**seulement**	only
faire	here: to offer	**supplément** m	surcharge
faire le plein	fill the tank	**toutes les**	both
forfait m	flat rate	**deux** f pl	
location f	rental	**toutes taxes**	all-inclusive
illimité	unlimited	**comprises (T.T.C.)**	
intéressant	interesting	**voiture de**	rental car
kilométrage m	mileage	**location** f	

Test 4

Work your way around the board. Each correct answer will take you to the next question until you have completed the exercise. Enjoy!

1
Choose one of the two answers. Then go to the square with the number of your answer.

2
Je travaille ... la journée.
toute ▸
8 tout ▸15

3
Wrong!
Go back to 5.

8
Correct! Continue:
Qu'est-ce que tu ... ?
dit ▸6
dis ▸25

9
Wrong!
Go back to 25.

10
Wrong!
Go back to 14.

11
Wrong!
Go back to 29.

16
Good! Continue:
Ils ... un disque.
offrent ▸22
offre ▸18

17
Wrong!
Go back to 22.

18
Wrong!
Go back to 16.

19
Correct!
End of exercise.

24
Wrong!
Go back to 12.

25
Very good! Continue:
Tu connais ce café ?
... café?
Quel ▸14
Quelle ▸9

26
Wrong!
Go back to 30.

27
Good! Continue:
Bonjour Claire, ça ...?
ira ▸23
va ▸12

4
Good! Continue:
... heure est-il ?
Quelle   ▶20
Quel   ▶7

5
Correct! Continue:
... prenez le petit
déjeuner.
Nous   ▶3
Vous   ▶13

6
Wrong!

Go back to 8.

7
Wrong!

Go back to 4.

12
Very good! Continue:
Le premier mai tombe
... un jeudi.   ▶16
jeudi.   ▶24

13
Correct! Continue:
Tu as ... âge?
quelle   ▶21
quel   ▶29

14
Very good! Continue:
Elle ouvre ... cadeau.
sa   ▶10
son   ▶30

15
Wrong!

Go back to 2.

20
Well done! Continue:
J'irai ... la Côte.
sur   ▶5
à   ▶28

21
Wrong!

Go back to 13.

22
Correct!
Mets ... les stages !
tout   ▶17
tous   ▶19

23
Wrong!

Go back to 27.

28
Wrong!

Go back to 20.

29
Well done! Continue:
Vous réglez ... espèces ?
en   ▶27
par   ▶11

30
Correct! Continue:
J'ai lu ... les annonces.
toutes   ▶4
tous   ▶26

day:21

The breakdown

Day 21 sees you dealing with an emergency situation. You will learn how to use the relative pronoun que, and how to use *venir de* to mean that you have just done something. You will also pick up some more vocabulary and useful cultural tips.

NUMBER PLATES...

The last two letters on French licence plates refer to the number of the **95 départements**, *which are in alphabetical sequence. Paris is in the* **département Seine** *(75),* **Grenoble, département Isère** *(38), etc. The postal code* **(indicatif)** *also includes the number of the* **département**. *For example, the postcode* **75011** *indicates an area within Paris as the first two numbers refer to* **département 75** *while the* **11** *stands for the* **arrondissement** *(quarter).*

French conversation: Panne sur l'autoroute

Claire et Denis reviennent de Normandie par l'autoroute A 13. Ils ont une panne.

Claire: Combien de kilomètres il y a encore jusqu'à Paris ?

Denis: On vient de passer la sortie pour Mantes-la-Jolie. Il reste environ une cinquante de kilomètres jusqu'au périphérique.

Claire: Tu entends ce drôle de bruit ? Qu'est-ce que ça peut bien être ?

Denis: Aucune idée. On dirait même que le bruit devient de plus en plus fort. Ça a l'air sérieux !

Claire: Arrête-toi sur le bas-côté ! On va appeler le service de dépannage. Je vais chercher une borne téléphonique. La dépanneuse arrive et le mécanicien inspecte la voiture.

Mécanicien: La courroie de transmission est complètement arrachée. Il faut la changer, mais je n'ai pas ce modèle avec moi. Je vais remorquer votre voiture jusqu'au prochain garage.

Denis: Quelle galère ! En plus, c'est une voiture que nous avons louée !

Mécanicien: Ne vous en faites pas ! L'agence de location vous remboursera les frais de réparation.

English conversation: Breakdown on the motorway

Claire and Denis are returning from Normandy on motorway A 13. Their car breaks down.

Claire: How many kilometres until Paris?

Denis: We just passed the Mantes-la-Jolie exit. We have about 50 kilometres left to the outer ring road (of Paris).

Claire: Do you hear that funny noise? What could that be?

Denis: Not a clue, but it seems to be getting louder. That sounds like something serious.

Claire: Stop on the hard shoulder! Let's call road service. I'll look for an emergency phone.

The road service arrives and the mechanic inspects the car.

Mechanic: The fan belt has been completely torn. It must be changed, but I don't have that type with me. I'll tow your car to the next garage.

Denis: What a nuisance! Especially with a rental car!

Mechanic: Don't worry! The car rental agency will reimburse you for the repair costs.

Grammar

The relative pronoun **que** (that/which/who) is a **direct object** that relates both to persons and objects. It can be left out in English but it must be included in French.

Que

C'est un acteur *que* je connais.	That's an actor (who) I know.
C'est un film *que* j'aime.	That's a movie (that) I like.
C'est l'exercice *qu'*elle a fait hier	That's the exercise (which) she did yesterday.

Note:
Que remains unchanged and becomes **qu'** before vowels.

The relative clause

Il lit un article qui est écrit en anglais.	He reads an article that is written in English.
J'ai une collègue qui parle italien.	I have a colleague who speaks Italian.
J'ai rencontré une stagiaire que vous connaissez.	I met a trainee whom you know.
La ville où j'habite est très belle.	The city in which I live is very nice.
Elle téléphone toujours à une heure où je ne suis pas au bureau.	She always phones at a time when I am not in the office.

In a relative clause the relative pronoun directly follows the noun to which it relates, e.g. in hte first example above, **qui** comes directly after **un article: Il lit un article qui est écrit en anglais.**
The relative pronoun **qui** (who/which/that) is the **subject** of the relative clause (see also Day 14) while **que** is a **direct object**.

In the fourth example, **La ville où j'habite est très belle, où** refers to a **place** or **time** specified in the main clause. In this case it refers to the place - the city.

venir de + infinitive

This construction is used to express an event that has happened just a few moments earlier.

Il vient de téléphoner.	He just called.

Exercises

Exercise 1

Insert qui or que.

1 C'est une voiture .... nous avons louée.

2 C'est l'agence .... remboursera les frais de réparation.

3 Mantes-la-Jolie est la sortie d'autoroute .... on vient de passer.

4 C'est la courroie de transmission .... est arrachée.

5 C'est le numéro de téléphone .... tu m'as donné.

6 C'est un livre .... est écrit en anglais.

7 J'ai rencontré dans la rue le client .... a téléphoné.

8 J'ai cherché la sortie d'autoroute .... est sur la carte.

9 C'est une chanteuse (female singer) .... j'aime beaucoup.

10 C'est la musique .... je préfère.

Exercise 2

Form sentences using the example given.

J'ai lu le journal.   *Je viens de lire le journal.*

1 Claire a téléphoné au service de dépannage.

....

2 Vous avez loué une voiture pour le week-end.

....

3 Ils ont passé la sortie d'autoroute.

....

4 Le mécanicien a réparé la voiture.

....

5 L'agence a remboursé les frais de réparation.

....

Excerise 3

Form sentences by joining up the correct halves.

1 C'est l'acteur que
2 Il reste 50 km
3 Aujourd'hui c'est Claire qui
4 Il va remorquer sa voiture
5 Je téléphone

a fait les courses.
b je préfère.
c jusqu'au périphérique.
d au service de dépannage.
e jusqu'au prochain garage.

1 .... 2 .... 3 .... 4 .... 5 ....

Exercice 4

Fill in the correct word.

a dépanneuse   b passer   c combien de   d bas-côté   e borne   f changer

1 .... kilomètres il y a encore jusqu'à Paris ?

2 On vient de .... la sortie pour Mantes-la-Jolie.

3 Arrête-toi sur le .... de la route.

4 Voilà une .... téléphonique.

5 La .... arrive.

6 Il faut .... la courroie de transmission.

Exercise 5

Translate:

Claire and Denis are returning from Normandy. 50 kilometres before (avant) Paris they have a car breakdown on the motorway. Claire calls the road service. The mechanic has to tow the car.

....

....

....

....

....

....

Vocabulary

Below is a list of vocabulary encountered in this chapter.

accélérateur m	throttle	**inspecter**	to inspect
accélérer	to accelerate	**klaxonner**	to honk
arraché	torn	**mécanicien** m	mechanic
aucun(e) idée	not a clue; no idea	**Ne vous en faites pas!**	Don't worry!
autoroute f	motorway/highway		
bas-côté m	(road) shoulder	**on dirait (dire)**	it seems
borne téléphonique f	emergency phone	**panne** f	breakdown
		passer	to pass (by)
bruit m	noise	**périphérique** m	motorway ring (road)
Ça a l'air sérieux !	That sounds serious!	**phares** m pl	lights/headlights
centre ville	city centre	**pleins phares**	high beam
changer	change	**pneu à plat** m	flat tyre Br/tire Am
complètement	completely	**pneu** m	tyre Br/tire Am
courroie de transmission f	fan belt	**Quelle galère!**	What a nuisance!
		ralentir	to slow down
cric m	jack	**rappel de**	traffic sign limitation
dépanneuse f	tow truck	**rembourser**	to reimburse
devenir	to become	**remorquer**	to tow
drôle	funny, odd	**réparer**	to repair
échangeur m	motorway intersection	**réservoir d'essence** m	petrol Br/gas Am
en codes m pl	with dimmed headlights		
en plus	in addition, besides	**revenir de**	to return
entendre	to hear	**service de dépannage** m	road service
environ	roughly, about		
essuie-glace m	windshield wiper	**sens unique**	one-way street
fort	strong	**sortie (d'autoroute)** f	(motorway) exit
frais de réparation m pl	repair costs		
		tank sens interdit	no entry
frein m	brake	**toutes directions**	all directions
freiner	to brake	**vitesse** f	speed
garage m	garage		

At the doctor's

Day 22 sees you take a visit to the doctors in France. You will learn how to conjugate the verb *croire* (to think/ believe) so you can express your opinions. You will also build up the vocabulary you need to talk about your health and you will learn more about the healthcare system in France.

MEDICAL SERVICES...

*For minor ailments, it is often worth making your local **pharmacy** (recognizable by its **green cross sign**) your first port of call. Pharmacies in France have wider prescribing powers than those in the UK or US. The standard of care in French hospitals is generally high. There is also a private, English-speaking hospital in Paris. The American Hospital is located at 63 Boulevard Victor-Hugo, 92292 Neuilly. Rates are more expensive than state-run hospitals.*

French conversation: Chez le médecin

Docteur: Bonjour, Mademoiselle. Qu'est-ce qui ne va pas ?
Claire: Je ne me sens pas bien. J'ai mal à la tête, je tousse et j'ai des
                frissons. J'ai l'impression que j'ai pris froid.
Docteur: Avez-vous de la fièvre ?
Claire: Oui, je crois.
Docteur: Allongez-vous, je vais vous ausculter.

Le docteur examine Claire.

Docteur: Vous avez une belle bronchite. Ce n'est pas étonnant ... Avec ce
                froid, tout le monde est malade. Vous pouvez vous rhabiller. Je
                vais vous donner quelque chose contre la fièvre. Vous prenez ce
                médicament trois fois par jour après les repas. Ensuite, du sirop.
                Prenez-en une cuillerée à soupe plusieurs fois par jour. Je vous
                conseille de rester au lit quelques jours. Voilà l'ordonnance et la
                feuille de maladie.
Claire: Merci Docteur, mais je suis anglaise et je ne suis pas assurée en
                France.
Docteur: La feuille de maladie vous servira de facture pour le
                remboursement des frais médicaux et pharmaceutiques dans votre
                pays.
Claire: Je vous dois combien pour la consultation ?
Docteur: €20, s'il vous plaît. Si ça ne va pas mieux à la fin de la semaine,
                revenez me voir, je vous donnerai des antibiotiques.

English conversation: At the doctor's

Doctor:	Good afternoon. What's wrong with you?
Claire:	I don't feel well. I have a headache, I'm coughing and I'm shivering. I think I've caught a cold.
Doctor:	Are you feverish?
Claire:	Yes, I think so.
Doctor:	Lie down, I want to listen to your chest.

The doctor examines Claire.

Doctor:	You have a fine bout of bronchitis. No wonder. In this kind of cold weather everybody is sick. You can get dressed again. I'll give you something for the fever. Take this medication three times a day after meals and take this cough syrup as well. Take one spoon up to four times a day. I'd also suggest you stay in bed for a few days. Here's the prescription and your sick form.
Claire:	Thank you, doctor, but I am English and I'm not insured in France.
Doctor:	The form can also be used as a receipt for the reimbursement of medical and pharmaceutical costs in your own country.
Claire:	How much do I owe you for the consultation?
Doctor:	€20, please. If you don't feel better by the end of the week, come and see me again and I'll give you some antibiotics.

Grammar

Conjunctions

Que (that) can be used as a conjunction in French to introduce an object clause. In English, the conjunction 'that' is often ommited, e.g. I think she is in Cannes.

Je crois qu'elle est à Cannes.	I think (that) she is in Cannes.
Il dit que Claire est malade.	He said (that) Claire is sick.
Elle raconte qu'elle a mal à la tête.	She said (that) she had a headache.

Verbs: croire (to believe, to think)

present tense	
je crois	nous croyons
tu crois	vous croyez
il/elle/on croit	ils/elles croient

perfect tense		
j'ai cru	tu as cru	il a cru

imperfect tense		
je croyais	tu croyais	il croyait

future tense		
je croirai	tu croiras	il croira

Exercises

Exercise 1

Using the following example, form sentences with que.

Claire est malade. Le médecin (dire que) ....   *Le médecin dit que Claire est malade.*

1 Claire a mal à la tête. Elle (dire que)

....

2 Claire tousse. Elle (raconter que)

....

3 Elle a pris froid. Elle (croire que)

....

4 Claire est assurée en Angleterre. Elle (dire que)

....

5 Les frais médicaux sont remboursés. Le médecin (dire que)

....

6 La consultation coûte 20 euros. Le médecin (dire que)

....

7 Claire a une bronchite. Le médecin (dire que)

....

8 Avec ce froid, tout le monde est malade. Le médecin (dire que)

....

Exercise 2

Fill in the present tense form of croire.

1 Tu (croire) .... qu'elle est à Paris?

2 Je (croire) .... qu'il va prendre les billets à la gare.

3 Vous (croire) .... qu'elle parle japonais?

4 Nous (croire) .... que c'est un bon médecin.

5 Il (croire) .... qu'il a une bronchite.

Excerise 3

Join up the questions with the correct answers:

1 Qu'est-ce qui ne va pas ?

2 Vous avez de la fièvre ?

3 Vous voulez prendre des antibiotiques ?

4 Je vous dois combien pour la consultation ?

a Non, je préfère attendre pour en prendre.

b J'ai mal à la tête, je tousse.

c 20 euros, s'il vous plaît.

d Oui, je crois.

1 .... **2** .... **3** .... **4** .... **5** ....

Exercise 4

One word in each line is out of place. Which one?

1 tousser	malade	fièvre	bonjour
2 facture	médicament	antibiotique	sirop
3 ordonnance	frais médicaux	repas	rembourser
4 par jour	mal à la tête	frissons	bronchite

1 .... **2** .... **3** .... **4** ....

Exercise 5

Translate the following text into French:

I think I've caught a cold. Could you give me a prescription (faire une ordonnance) for some antibiotics? Take this medication three times a day. Stay in bed for a few days. If you're not getting better come see me next week.

....

....

....

....

....

....

Vocabulary

Below is a list of vocabulary encountered in this chapter.

antibiotique *m*	*antibiotics*
après	*after*
assuré	*insured*
ausculter	*to listen to one's chest/ breathing*
avoir des frissons	*to have shivering fits*
avoir mal à la tête	*to have a headache*
bronchite f	*bronchitis*
cachet *m*	*tablet, pill*
consultation *f*	*consultation*
cuillerée *f*	*a spoonful*
douleur *f*	*pain*
étonnant	*surprising*
examiner	*to examine*
facture *f*	*invoice, bill*
feuille de	*accounting form (for*
maladie *f*	*insurance)*
faire une ordonnance	*to write a prescription*
frais médicaux *m pl*	*medical costs*
frais pharmaceutiques *m pl*	*cost for medications*
froid *m*	*cold*
heures de consultation *f pl*	*consultation hours*

impression *f*	*impression*
malade	*sick, ill*
malade *m f*	*person who is sick/ill*
médicament *m*	*medication, medicine*
médecin *m*	*doctor*
mieux	*better*
ordonnance *f*	*prescription*
pas bien	*not good*
pharmacien *m*	*pharmacist*
piqûre *f*	*syringe, injection*
prendre froid	*to catch a cold*
prescrire	*to write a prescription*
remboursement *m*	*reimbursement*
repas *m*	*meal*
rester au lit	*to stay in bed*
s'allonger	*to lie down*
se rhabiller	*to get dressed again*
se sentir	*to feel*
se déshabiller	*to get undressed*
spécialiste *m*	*specialist (doctor)*
sirop *m*	*cough syrup*
tousser	*to cough*
tout le monde	*everybody*

day:23

Camping

Day 23 sees you go on a camping trip over a bank holiday weekend. This chapter will also teach you how to use en + present participle, as well as the past participle to describe events that have happened more fluently. You will also further increase your vocabulary.

REGIONAL CULTURES...

France has many regional languages and plenty of customs and traditions. Some quaint customs include giving lilies of the valley as a present on May 1st and the saying that if you have the last drop drop of wine from a bottle, you will be married within the year. Some of the regional languages include: **Occitan** *(Provençal) in the south,* **Catalan** *and* **Basque** *along the border with Spain,* **Breton** *in Brittany (bumper stickers with* **Breiz** *=* **Bretagne***) and the* **Alsatian** *dialect spoken in the Alsace region bordering Germany.*

French conversation: Camping en Provence

Claire est partie en voiture avec les Rougier dans le Massif du Lubéron en Provence pour y passer le week-end du 1er mai.

Michel:	Quelle chance que le premier mai tombe un jeudi ! Ça nous permet de partir quatre jours !
Caroline:	Apt, 10 km, nous sommes presque arrivés. Saignon n'est qu'à 5 km d'Apt. Tu vas voir, c'est un superbe village, entouré de champs de lavande.
Michel:	Oui, mais ce n'est pas encore la saison! La lavande ne fleurit qu'en juillet. Mai, c'est le mois du muguet !
Caroline:	Là, tourne à droite! Camping »A qui sian ben«.
Michel:	Tiens regarde, les tarifs sont affichés. Emplacement tente €10 la nuit, supplément voiture e4.
Claire:	Qu'est-ce que ça veut dire »A qui sian ben« ?
Caroline:	C'est du provençal: »Ici on est bien« ... Allons-y ! Bonjour, Monsieur,vous avez de la place pour deux tentes ?
Gardien:	Pas de problème à cette saison ! Installez-vous où vous voulez. Les sanitaires se trouvent derrière la réception. Ça vous convient ?
Caroline:	Magnifique, quel calme !
Gardien:	Vous voulez rester combien de jours ?
Michel:	Trois nuits, nous partirons dimanche dans l'après-midi.
Gardien:	Parfait. Profitez du soleil de Provence. Vous payerez en partant, n'oubliez pas hein ?
Claire:	On monte les tentes avant la nuit ?
Michel:	Bonne idée, ah zut! J'ai oublié ma lampe de poche !
Caroline:	J'en ai une. Heureusement que je pense à tout, à la lampe de poche, aux sacs de couchage, au camping-gaz ... Au fait, j'espère que tu as pris le marteau pour planter les piquets.
Michel:	Non, j'ai oublié. Mais une grosse pierre fera l'affaire !

English conversation: Camping in Provence

Claire drove with the Rougiers to the Lubéron Massif in Provence to spend the May 1st bank holiday weekend there.

Michel:	We are really lucky that the 1st of May falls on a Thursday. We can go away for four days!
Caroline:	Apt, 10 kilometres, we're nearly there. Saignon is not even 5 kilometres away from Apt. You'll soon see, a delightful village surrounded by lavender fields.
Michel:	Yes, that's true, but it isn't the season for it yet. Lavender doesn't bloom until July. May is the month for lily of the valley.
Caroline:	There, turn right! Camping "A qui sian ben".
Michel:	Look, there's a price list posted. To pitch a tent is €10 per night and an extra €4 for the car.
Claire:	What does "A qui sian ben" mean?
Caroline:	That's Provençal and means "A good place to be" ... Let's go! Hi, have you got space left for two tents?
Guard:	No problem at this time of year! Pitch your tents wherever you want. The bathrooms are behind the reception. Do you like it here?
Caroline:	It's great, so peaceful!
Guard:	How many days will you be staying?
Michel:	For three nights, we'll leave on Sunday afternoon.
Guard:	Perfect. Enjoy the Provence sunshine. You pay when you leave, but don't forget, OK?
Claire:	Shall we pitch the tents before it's dark?
Michel:	Good idea! Drat, I forgot my flashlight!
Caroline:	I have one. Luckily, I thought of everything, the flashlight, the sleeping bags, the camping stove ... By the way, I assume that you brought the hammer for the tent pegs.
Michel:	No I forgot. But a big stone will also do!

En + present participle

The present participle is formed by adding the ending -ant to the stem of the first person plural of the present tense, e.g. **nous arrivons**, present participle **arrivant**. This is the case for all verbs.

The gerund **en + present participle** expresses a concurrent event as in:
elle écoute la radio *en* **fais***ant* **la cuisine** - she listens to the radio while cooking.
The gerund can also describe the circumstantial reasons for something happening as in:
il s'est cassé la jambe *en* **fais***ant* **du ski** - he broke his lwg while skiing.

Vous payerez *en* part*ant*.	You (will) pay before you leave (before leaving).
Elle écoute la radio *en* fais*ant* la cuisine.	While cooking she listens to the radio.
Il s'est cassé la jambe *en* fais*ant* du ski.	He broke his leg skiing.
Elle a appris le français *en* travaill*ant* en France.	She learned French when she worked in France.

Past participle

a) The past participle of verbs, whose perfect tense is formed with **être** (see Day 7), agrees in gender and number with the **subject** of the sentence to which it relates.

Nous sommes arrivés.	We have arrived.

b) The past participle of verbs, whose perfect tense is formed with **avoir**, agrees in gender and number with the direct object if it **precedes** the verb.

These direct objects can precede the verb in the form of personal pronouns: **le, la, les, me, te, nous, vous**:

J'ai oublié *la tente*.	I forgot the tent.
Je *l'*ai oublié*e*.	I forgot it.
J'ai oublié *les papiers de la voiture*.	I forgot the car documents.
Je *les* ai oublié*s*.	I forgot them.
Il *nous* a invité*s*.	He has invited us.

– relative pronoun **que**:

C'est *la voiture que* j'ai loué*e*.	That's the car (that) I hired.

– interrogative determiner **quel**:

J'ai réservé les chambres.	I reserved the rooms.
Quelles chambres as-tu réservé*es*?	Which rooms did you reserve?

– *combien de* + noun at the start of an interrogative clause:

Combien de chambres as-tu réservé*es* ?	How many rooms did you reserve?

Exercises

Exercise 1

Form sentences using the following example.

Apprenez le français ! (écouter la radio)   *Apprenez le français en écoutant la radio !*

1 Trouvez un appartement! (mettre une annonce dans le journal).

....

2 Perdez 5 kilos! (loose 5 kilograms of weight) (faire du sport).

....

3 Montez la tente! (arriver au camping).

....

4 N'oubliez pas votre lampe de poche! (partir).

....

5 Téléphone à Miko! (rentrer à Paris).

....

Exercise 2

Join the sentences together as in the following example.

Elle travaille. Elle écoute la radio.   *Elle travaille en écoutant la radio.*

1 Ils dînent. Ils regardent la télé (they watch TV).

....

2 Il s'est blessé (he has injured himself). Il a monté la tente.

....

3 Ils ont oublié de payer. Ils sont partis.

....

4 Claire a rencontré Denis. Elle est allée à Grenoble.

....

5 Nous avons trouvé le camping. Nous sommes arrivés à Apt.

....

Exercise 3

Fill in the correct ending of the past participle.

1 Nous sommes arrivé............. le soir au camping.

2 Ils sont resté............. trois jours à Apt.

3 Elle est venu............. en Provence à Pâques.

4 Ils sont allé............. à Aix-en-Provence.

5 Claire est parti............. en voiture avec Michel et Caroline.

Exercise 4

Join up the questions with the correct answers.

1 Vous voulez rester combien de jours ?   **a** Bonne idée !

2 Vous avez de la place pour deux tentes ?   **b** Trois nuits.

3 On monte les tentes avant la nuit ?   **c** C'est du provençal.

4 Qu'est-ce que ça veut dire »A qui sian ben« ?   **d** Pas de problème à cette saison.

1.........   2.........   3.........   4.........

Exercise 5

One word in each line is out of place. Which one?

1	lavande	muguet	rose	mai
2	sac de couchage	tarif	lampe de poche	marteau
3	juillet	saison	août	septembre
4	piquet	gardien	camping-gaz	tente

1..........................   2..........................   3..........................   4..........................

Exercise 6

Translate the following into French:

We are nearly there. Saignon is not even five kilometres away from Apt. We have space for two tents. We pitch the tents. We forgot the torch/flashlight and the hammer.

....

....

....

....

....

....

Vocabulary

Below is a list of vocabulary encountered in this chapter.

affiché	*displayed, posted*	**parfait**	*perfect, great*
camping-gaz *m*	*camping stove*	**payer**	*to pay*
champ de	*lavender field*	**penser à**	*to think of (doing*
lavande *m*			*something)*
convenir	*to be suitable*	**permettre**	*to enable, to permit*
emplacement	*tent site*	**pierre** *f*	*stone*
tente *m*		**piquet** *m*	*tent peg*
en partant	*when leaving*	**planter**	*to insert, to plant*
entouré de	*surrounded by*	**presque**	*almost*
faire du camping	*to camp*	**profiter de**	*to enjoy, make the most of*
faire l'affaire	*to do the job,*	**s'installer**	*to settle down, install*
	(it will do the job)		*onself*
fleurir	*to bloom*	**sac de couchage** *m*	*sleeping bag*
camping *m*	*camping*	**saison** *f*	*season*
gardien	*guard, administrator*	**sanitaires** *f pl*	*bathrooms*
(du camping) *m*		**soleil** *m*	*sun*
gros	*fat, big*	**superbe**	*superb, great*
hein	*isn't it?/OK*	**tarif** *m*	*price, rate*
heureusement	*luckily, happily*	**tente** *f*	*tent*
lampe de poche	*flashlight*	**terrain de**	*camping site*
le 1er mai	*May 1st*	**camping** *m*	
marteau *m*	*hammer*	**tomber**	*to fall*
monter une	*to pitch a tent*	**village** *m*	*village*
tente		**Zut !**	*Damn!/Drat!*
oublier	*to forget*		

day:24

Markets

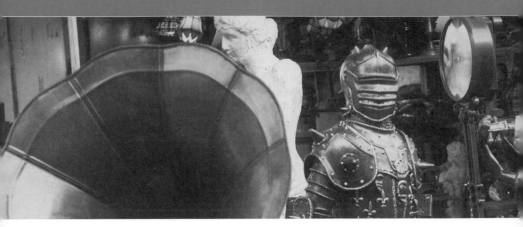

Day 24 introduces French markets. You will also learn how to make more sophisticated sentences using negatives and you will learn some nouns with irregular plural forms. Practice what you have learnt using the exercises at the end of the chapter.

FLEA MARKETS...

*Famous Parisian flea markets that are open at the weekend are in **Montreuil** and in **Saint Ouen**. In Montreuil the market is open Saturdays and Sunday morning. The market in Saint Ouen is open all day Saturday, Sunday and Monday. They are within easy reach of Paris by subway - Saint Ouen is the last stop on the **métro Porte de Clignancourt** and **Montreuil** is near **métro Mairie de Montreuil**.*

French conversation: Les Puces

Claire et Miko sont aux Puces de Saint Ouen.

Vendeur:	Alors mes petites dames, on n'achète rien aujourd'hui ? Regardez-moi ces foulards, pure soie !
Claire:	C'est combien ?
Vendeur:	4 € pièce, les deux pour sept. Un pour chacune ! Allez, un petit cadeau!
Miko:	Non merci, on vient juste d'arriver. On voudrait faire un tour avant d'acheter.
Claire:	Oh, regarde les chapeaux Miko ! Celui-ci est vraiment drôle. Ma grand-mère avait le même quand elle était jeune. Essaie-le !
Miko:	Non, je n'ose pas. Je ne le mettrai jamais ! Ça fait complètement ringard !
Claire:	Pas du tout, tout à fait 1925, je suis sûre que ça te va à merveille !

Miko essaie le chapeau.

Vendeur:	Tenez, voilà une glace. Ça vous va très bien, la classe !
Miko:	Il est pas mal, mais un peu décousu! Vous le vendez combien ?
Vendeur:	Allez ! Je vous fais un prix ! 50 € !
Claire:	50 € ! C'est plus cher qu'aux Galeries Lafayette !
Miko:	C'est trois fois trop cher! Dommage ! Au revoir !
Vendeur:	Attendez, ne partez pas comme ça ! Je vous le laisse à 48 € !
Miko:	Je vous donne 40 €, pas plus !
Vendeur:	42 € et il est à vous.
Miko:	Ecoutez, je vais réfléchir !

English conversation: The flea market

Claire and Miko are at the flea market of Saint Ouen.

Vendor:	So my dears, not buying anything today? Look at these scarves, pure silk!
Claire:	How much are they?
Vendor:	€4 each, two for € 7. One for each of you! Come on, a little present!
Miko:	No thanks, we've just arrived. We want to look around before we buy anything.
Claire:	Look at these hats, Miko! This one is really funny. My grandmother had the same ones when she was young. Try it on!
Miko:	No, I wouldn't dare. I'll never wear it! It looks really old fashioned.
Claire:	Not at all, it's twenties style. I am sure it'll suit you perfectly!

Miko tries on the hat.

Vendor:	Here's a mirror. It suits you really well; it's really stylish!
Miko:	It's not bad, but the seams are coming apart! How much are you asking for it?
Vendor:	Well, I'll make you a good price: €50!
Claire:	€50! That's more expensive than the Galeries Lafayette!
Miko:	That's three times as much! What a pity! Goodbye!
Vendor:	Wait, don't walk away like that! I'll give it to you for €48.
Miko:	I'll give you €40, and not a cent more!
Vendor:	42 and its yours.
Miko:	Listen, I'll think about it!

Grammar

Nouns with irregular plural forms

Generally the plural of a noun is formed by adding an -s to the singular (see Day 2). There are a number of nouns, though, whose plural does not end with -s and instead ends in -aux and -x

nouns with -al	*singular*	*plural*
	le journ*al*	les journ*aux*
with -au		
	le noy*au*	les noy*aux* (pits)
with -eau		
	le chap*eau*	les chap*eaux*
	le cad*eau*	les cad*eaux*
	le bur*eau*	les bur*eaux*
with -ail		
	le trav*ail*	les trav*aux*
with -eu		
	le j*eu*	les j*eux* (games)
with -ou		
	le gen*ou*	les gen*oux* (knees)

The negative in compound tenses

You have already learnt that the negative consists of two parts, which enclose the conjugated verb (see Day 6). With compound tenses, the two parts of the negative enclose the conjugated auxiliary verbs avoir or être.

Tu as acheté quelque chose aux Puces ?	Did you buy anything at the flea market?
Non, je *n'*ai *rien* acheté.	No, I didn't buy anything.
Tu es venue en bus ?	Did you come by bus?
Non, je *ne* suis *pas* venue en bus.	No, I didn't come by bus.

Exercises

Exercise 1

Fill in the correct plural ending.

1 Nous organisons les voyage......... d'affaires.

2 J'ai trente jour......... de vacances par an.

3 L'agence a loué des bureau......... à Marseille.

4 Il n'aime pas les jeu......... de cartes (deck of cards).

5 On peut acheter des (journal)......... anglais à Nice.

6 On m'a offert beaucoup de cadeau......... pour mon anniversaire.

7 Il a acheté deux marteau......... pour planter les piquets de tente.

8 Claire et Miko ont acheté des chapeau......... aux Puces.

Exercise 2

Create sentences in the past tense using the following example.

Je n'achète (acheté) rien aux Puces.   *Je n'ai rien acheté aux Puces.*

1 Elle ne prend pas le métro (pris).

....

2 Il ne rencontre jamais Abel (rencontré).

....

3 Tu ne téléphones plus à 11 heures (téléphoné).

....

4 Elle ne met pas de jeans (mis).

....

5 Je ne vends rien (vendu).

....

6 Elle ne va pas à Londres (allé).

....

7 Nous n'arrivons pas lundi (arrivé).

....

8 Tu ne dis plus bonjour (dit).

....

9 Je ne travaille jamais le dimanche (travaillé).

....

10 Tu n'aimes pas ce film (aimé).

....

Exercise 3

One word in each line is out of place. Which one?

1	cadeau	chapeau	marteau	combien
2	jeune	drôle	dommage	cher
3	essayer	acheter	soie	mettre
4	foulard	glace	pull	jean
5	grand-mère	vendeur	client	marché

1..................... 2................. 3................. 4................. 5.................

Exercise 4

Translate the following text into French:

I'd like to look around first. Try on this hat! How much are you asking for it? That's too expensive! I'll think about it.

....

....

....

....

....

....

Vocabulary

Below is a list of vocabulary encountered in this chapter.

à merveille	wonderful	**jean** m	jeans
avant de	before	**jeune**	young
cadeau m	gift, present	**la classe**	stylish
chacun(e)	each, everyone	**laisser pour**	to leave, let
chapeau m	hat	**même**	the same
décousu	undone, unstitched	**oser**	to dare
Dommage !	What a pity!	**pas mal**	not bad
drôle	funny	**pièce** f	piece
écouter	to hear	**quand**	when, whenever
faire un prix	to make a good price	**réfléchir**	to think reflect on
faire un tour	to look around	**regarder**	to look at
foulard m	scarf	**ringard**	old fashioned
les Puces f pl	flea market	**sûr**	certain, sure
glace f	mirror	**vendeur** m	vendor, seller
grand-mère f	grandmother	**vraiment**	actually/real(ly)
grand-père m	grandfather		

Making plans

Day 25 introduces you to the subjunctive mood. You will continue to improve your comprehension and conversation skills and by now you will be comfortable in a variety of different situations.

GESTURES...

*Now that you are familiar with speaking French, try to become more accustomed to French gestures which often speak a thousand words. The French repertoire of gestures is extensive and varied, and many will have no cultural significance in your home country. For example, using an index finger to pull down the lower eyelid is to say **Mon œil !** (literally My eye!) or I dont believe you!, while bringing a fist up to your mouth and tapping it back and forth means **Complètement bourré !** (litterally filled up) or You're drunk!*

French conversation: Organiser un voyage d'affaires

Denis:	Le patron a décidé de nous envoyer cette année au Festival International du Film publicitaire qui a lieu à Cannes.
Claire:	A quelle date ?
Denis:	C'est du 19 au 24 juin. Tu dois t'occuper de réserver les billets d'avion et l'hôtel.
Claire:	Nous resterons combien de jours ?
Denis:	En tout quatre jours. On arrivera le samedi soir et on repartira le mercredi matin avec le premier vol sur Paris.

Denis sort du bureau, Claire téléphone à un hôtel à Cannes.

Claire:	Allô ! Claire Dietz de l'agence Charrain à Paris. Je vous téléphone pour une réservation. Je voudrais deux chambres individuelles avec salle de bains, si possible côté cour, du 17 au 20 juin.
Réceptioniste:	Nous sommes presque complet à cause du festival de pub, mais attendez un instant, je vais regarder ce qu'il reste ... Allô ? Désolée, mais il nous reste deux chambres individuelles côté cour mais avec douche.
Claire:	Vous n'avez plus du tout de chambre avec salle de bains ?
Réceptioniste:	Si, mais ce sont des chambres pour deux personnes.
Claire:	Alors réservez les deux chambres individuelles s'il vous plaît.
Réceptioniste:	D'accord. Il faut que vous nous confirmiez votre réservation par fax. Mentionnez s'il vous plaît votre heure d'arrivée approximative à l'hôtel.

English conversation: Organizing a business trip

Denis:	The boss has decided to send us to the International Advertisement Film Festival in Cannes this year.
Claire:	When?
Denis:	From June 19th to 24th. You have to take care of the flight and hotel reservations.
Claire:	How many days will we be staying?
Denis:	Altogether four days. We'll arrive on Saturday evening and we'll fly back to Paris on the first plane on Wednesday morning.

Denis leaves the office; Claire calls a hotel in Cannes.

Claire:	Hello. This is Claire Dietz from the Charrain Agency in Paris. I am calling to make a reservation. I'd like two single rooms with bathrooms from June 17th to 20th, if possible facing the back.
Receptionist:	We're almost full because of the ad festival but hold on one minute, I'll check what we have left ... Hello? I'm sorry, but we only have two single rooms with showers facing the back left.
Claire:	You don't have any rooms with a bath left?
Receptionist:	Yes we do, but they are all double rooms.
Claire:	Please reserve those two single rooms then.
Receptionist:	OK. You'll have to confirm your reservation by fax. Please indicate your approximate time of arrival at the hotel.

Grammar

il faut que + subjunctive

The subjunctive mood is used to express various states such as wishes, emotions, possibility, judgment, opinions, necessities, or actions that have **not yet** occurred. In English it is seldom used. The sentence that follows Il faut que takes the subjunctive. The subjunctive is also used after pour que (that, in order that) and after a number of verbs.

Il faut que vous *confirmiez* votre réservation.
You have to confirm your reservation.

Present subjunctive: verbs ending in *-er*

Il faut que *je* réserve une chambre.
Il faut que *tu* téléphones à Cannes.
Il faut qu'*elle* demande un visa.
Il faut que *nous* arrivions à 8 heures.
Il faut que *vous* confirmiez votre réservation.
Il faut qu'*ils* organisent leur voyage.

Note:
Verbs ending in -er have the same endings in the subjunctive as in the present tense (see Day 1) except for nous and vous. A subjunctive clause is usually preceded by que.

il faut + infinitive, il faut que + subjunctive

Il faut (one has to/it is necessary) can be used in two ways:
It can be used with an infinitive without a preposition as shown in example 1 below.
If it is followed by que, it must take the subjunctive, as shown in example 2 below.
Both constructions are widely used and have the same meaning.

1. Il faut confirmer votre réservation.
2. Il faut que vous confirmiez votre réservation.

Exercises

Exercise 1

Using the following example, fill in the present subjunctive.

Il faut que (vous réserver) deux chambres. *Il faut que vous réserviez deux chambres.*

1 Il faut que (vous organiser) .... le voyage d'affaires.

2 Il faut que (vous téléphoner) .... à l'hôtel aujourd'hui.

3 Il faut que (vous arriver) .... samedi soir à Cannes.

4 Il faut que (vous rencontrer) .... vos clients lundi et mardi.

5 Il faut que (vous travailler) .... beaucoup le week-end.

Exercise 2

Rewrite the sentences using the following example.

Il faut que nous arrivions le matin. *Il faut arriver le matin.*

1 Il faut que nous cherchions son numéro de téléphone.

....

2 Il faut que nous demandions la date du festival.

....

3 Il faut que nous présentions notre agence.

....

4 Il faut que nous réservions deux chambres à l'hôtel.

....

5 Il faut que nous pensions à réserver le vol de retour.

....

Exercise 3

What do you say if you . . .

1 . . . want a double room with a bath?   **1** ....

   a Je voudrais une chambre pour deux personnes avec salle de bains.

   b Je voudrais deux chambres avec douche.

2 . . . want a book from July 14th to 20th?   **2** ....

   a quatorze à vingt juillet.   **b** du quatorze au vingt juillet.

3 . . . want a room facing the back?   **3** ....

   a côté rue   **b** côté cour

4 . . . want confirm your reservation by email?   **4** ....

   a Je vous envoie un email.   **b** Je vous confirme ma réservation par email.

Exercice 4

Complete the sentences by filling in qui or que (see Days 14 and 21).

1 C'est Claire .... téléphone à un hôtel à Cannes et ....fait les réservations.

2 Denis et Claire vont au festival International du Film publicitaire .... a lieu tous les ans à Cannes.

3 Les chambres .... Claire a réservées sont avec douche.

4 Monsieur Charrain .... est le directeur de l'agence, n'ira ....pas à Cannes.

5 C'est la secrétaire .... a l'adresse .... vous cherchez.

6 Le fax .... vous avez envoyé hier est arrivé ce matin.

7 Ils aiment beaucoup le travail .... ils font à l'agence.

8 Monsieur Hituschi? C'est un client ....je n'ai pas encore rencontré.

9 C'est l'agence .... payera tous les frais de voyage ....(travel expenses).

10 Je n'ai pas trouvé le plan de Cannes .... tu cherchais.

11 Ce n'est pas le coup de fil ....j'attendais !

12 Tu connais ce collègue .... travaille pour nous à Lyon ?

Exercise 5

Translate:

Hi. This is Claire Dietz from the Binet agency in Paris. I'd like to reserve two single rooms with bathrooms from the 2nd to the 8th of May. I have to confirm my reservation by email.

....

....

....

....

....

Vocabulary

Below is a list of vocabulary encountered in this chapter.

à cause de	because of, due to	**il faut que vous**	you must/have to
approximatif	roughly, approximately	**instant** m	moment
arrivée f	arrival	**mentionner**	to specify, mention
avion m	airplane	**organiser**	to organize
avoir lieu	to take place	**plus du tout**	nothing more
billet d'avion m	airline ticket	**regarder**	to look
ce que	what, which	**repartir**	to leave (again)
cette année	this year	**réservation** f	reservation
chambre individuelle f	single room	**réserver**	to reserve, book
		rester	to remain, stay (behind)
chambre pour deux personnes f	double room	**s'occuper de**	to take care of
		salle de bains f	bathroom, (bath)
complet	full, booked out	**si**	if; yes (in answer to a negative question only)
confirmer	to confirm		
côté cour	facing the back	**si possible**	if possible
décider	to decide	**sortir (de)**	to leave
désolé m	I'm sorry	**vol aller** m	outgoing flight
desolée f		**vol** m	flight
en tout	in total	**vol retour** m	return flight
envoyer	to send	**voyage d'affaires** m	business trip
heure f	time (of day)		

Test 5

Work your way around the board. Each correct answer will take you to the next question until you have completed the exercise. Enjoy!

1

Choose one of the two answers and go to the square with the number of your answer.

2

Elle a mal ... tête.
à la   ▶8
au   ▶15

3

Wrong!

Go back to 5.

8

Correct! Continue:
Vous restez ... jours?
combien   ▶6
combien de   ▶25

9

Wrong!

Go back to 25.

10

Wrong!

Go back to 14.

11

Wrong!

Go back to 29.

16

Good! Continue:
Je n'ai rien ...
vendu.   ▶22
vendre.   ▶18

17

Wrong!

Go back to 22.

18

Wrong!

Go back to 16.

19

Correct!
End of exercise

24

Wrong!

Go back to 12.

25

Very good! Continue:
Vous avez ... une voiture?
loué   ▶14
louer   ▶9

26

Wrong!

Go back to 30.

27

Good! Continue:
Ils ... restés 3 jours.
ont   ▶23
sont   ▶12

4
Good! Continue:
Il y a ... place pour deux tentes?
de la   ▶20
du   ▶7

5
Correct! Continue:
Vous payerez ...
partant?   ▶3
en partant?   ▶13

6
Wrong!

Go back to 8.

7
Wrong!

Go back to 4.

12
Very good! Continue:
Elle est ... en voiture.
partie   ▶16
parti   ▶24

13
Correct! Continue:
Ils sont ... à Arles.
allé   ▶21
allés   ▶29

14
Very good! Continue:
J'ai acheté deux ...
chapeau   ▶10
chapeaux   ▶30

15
Wrong!

Go back to 2.

20
Well done! Continue:
C'est l'acteur ... je préfère.
que   ▶5
qui   ▶28

21
Wrong!

Go back to 13.

22
Correct!
C'est la route ... va à Apt.
que   ▶17
qui   ▶19

23
Wrong!

Go back to 27.

28
Wrong!

Go back to 20.

29
Well done! Continue:
Ca te va très ...
bien.   ▶27
bon.   ▶11

30
Correct! Continue:
C'est une ville ... j'adore.
que   ▶4
qui   ▶26

day:26

At the beach

Day 26 discusses the weather and introduces you to the conditional tense (what you would like to do). You will also learn how to conjugate the verb *pouvoir* (to be able to/can) and build up your holiday vocabulary.

CANNES...

The annual Cannes Film Festival (Festival de Cannes) held in May each year was begun in the late 1940s to rival the competition held in Venice. Today, it has consolidated the town's reputation for glamor and celebrity-spotting. Head along the fashion-conscious promenade, the palm-lined Boulevard de la Croisette with its luxury hotels, galleries and boutiques. For the most spectacular view, head up to the Observatoire de Super-Cannes, north of the Pointe.

French conversation: A la plage

A Cannes plage de la Croisette.

Claire:	Tu devrais te mettre de la crème solaire.
Denis:	Tu crois, pourquoi ?
Claire:	Parce que tu as déjà un coup de soleil. Tu es tout rouge. On se fait bronzer depuis deux heures. On pourrait faire autre chose !
Denis:	Il est presque trois heures. On pourrait prendre le bateau pour les îles de Lérins.
Claire:	Qu'est-ce qu'il y a à voir aux îles de Lérins ?
Denis:	Il y deux îles, Sainte-Marguerite et Saint-Honorat. C'est très calme. On pourrait faire une balade dans la forêt d'eucalyptus et visiter le monastère.
Claire:	La traversée dure longtemps ?
Denis:	Non, 20 minutes ou une demi-heure.
Claire:	Bon, je retourne me changer à l'hôtel, tu passeras me chercher dans une heure ?
Denis:	D'accord, je t'attendrai dans le hall.

English conversation: On the beach

In Cannes, Croisette Beach.

Claire:	You should put on some suntan lotion.
Denis:	You think so? Why?
Claire:	Because you already have sunburn. You are all red. We've been lying in the sun for two hours now. We could do something different!
Denis:	It is nearly three o'clock. We could take the boat to the Lérins Islands.
Claire:	What's there to see on the Lérins Islands?
Denis:	There are two islands, Sainte-Marguerite and Saint-Honorat. It's very peaceful there. We could take a walk through the eucalyptus forest and visit the monastery.
Claire:	Does the boat trip take long?
Denis:	No, 20 minutes or half an hour.
Claire:	Good, then I'll go back to the hotel and change. Can you pick me up in an hour?
Denis:	OK, I'll wait for you in the lobby.

Grammar

The weather

Quel temps fait-il ?	How is the weather?
Il fait beau (temps).	It's nice/fine.
Il fait mauvais temps.	It's bad.
Il fait du soleil.	It's sunny.
Il fait du vent.	It's windy.
Il fait chaud.	It's hot.
Il fait froid.	It's cold.
Il pleut.	It's rainy/raining.
Le temps est nuageux.	It's cloudy.

Conditional tense

The conditional tense is used for some polite expressions, such as **j'aimerais, je voudrais**. The conditional tense is also used to make a suggestion, as in **on pourrait** (one/we could).

J'aimerais aller à Nice.	I would like to go to Nice.
Je voudrais parler à Sarah.	I would like to speak to Sarah.
On pourrait prendre le bateau.	One/We could take the boat.

Pouvoir (to be able to, can)

present tense	
je peux	nous pouvons
tu peux	vous pouvez
il/elle peut	ils/elles peuvent

perfect tense
j'ai pu etc.

imperfect tense	
je pouvais	nous pouvions
tu pouvais	vous pouviez
il/elle pouvait	ils/elles pouvaient

future tense	
je pourrai	nous pourrons
tu pourras	vous pourrez
il/elle pourra	ils/elles pourront

conditional tense	
je pourrais	nous pourrions
tu pourrais	vous pourriez
il/elle/on pourrait	ils/elles pourraient

Conditional tense of verbs ending in -*er*

All regular verbs take the same endings in the conditional tense.
The conditional tense of verbs ending in **-er** and **-ir** is formed by taking the infinitive of the verb and adding the endings:
-ais, -ais, -ait, -ions, -iez, -aient.

For verbs ending in **-re**, you drop the **-re** and add the same endings as above:
-ais, -ais, -ait, -ions, -iez, -aient.

Aimer (to like/love)

conditional tense	
j'aime*rais*	nous aime*rions*
tu aime*rais*	vous aime*riez*
il/elle aime*rait*	ils/elles aime*raient*

Exercises

Exercise 1

Fill in the correct form of the verb in the conditional tense.

1 Nous (pouvoir) .... prendre le bateau vers 4 heures.

2 On (pouvoir) .... faire une balade dans la forêt.

3 Vous (pouvoir) .... me téléphoner mercredi ?

4 Je (pouvoir) .... passer vous chercher à l'hôtel.

5 Tu (pouvoir) .... me rendre un service ?

6 J'(aimer) .... aller au concert avec toi.

7 Qu'est-ce que tu (aimer) .... comme cadeau pour ton anniversaire ?

8 Vous (aimer) .... aller dans un restaurant japonais ?

9 Nous (aimer) .... louer une petite voiture.

10 Elle (aimer) .... aller au Japon l'année prochaine.

Exercise 2

Insert the appropriate object pronouns (see Days 10 and 11).

1 Vous connaissez ce pays ? Oui, je .... connais bien.

2 Vous avez déjà parlé à Monsieur Charrain ? Non, je ne .... ai pas encore parlé.

3 Tu feras ton voyage en Argentine en mai ? Non, je ne peux pas partir en mai, je .... ferai en juillet.

4 Où est-ce que tu as oublié tes lunettes ? Je .... ai oubliées dans le train au wagon-restaurant.

5 Tu as lu le dernier roman de Milan Kundera ? Non, je ne .... ai pas encore lu.

6 Vous avez loué cette voiture pour combien de temps ? Nous .... avons louée pour une semaine.

7 Vous aimez la Côte d'Azur ? Je ne .... connais pas !

8 Tu connais les acteurs de ce film? Oui, je .... connais tous !

9 Tu as demandé à Claire et à Denis de venir à quelle heure ?

Je .... ai demandé de venir à 8 heures.

10 Denis est arrivé au bureau ? Je ne sais pas, je ne .... ai pas encore vu.

11 Tu as acheté les journaux pour Miko ? Oui, je .... ai achetés hier à la gare.

Exercise 3

One word in each line is out of place. Which one?

1 plage	bronzer	soleil	neige
2 Marseille	Cannes	Paris	Nice
3 lavande	terre	rose	fleur
4 traversée	réunion	voyage	balade
5 rouge	vert	blanc	malade

1 .... 2 .... 3 .... 4 .... 5 ....

Exercise 5

Translate:

How is the weather? It is nice, I would like to go to the beach. Me too but I have to go to the bank first to change some money. OK, I'll pick you up in an hour.

....

....

....

....

....

....

Vocabulary

Below is a list of vocabulary encountered in this chapter.

banque f	bank	**(de bain)** m	
balade f	walk, stroll	**monastère** m	monastery
calme	calm, quiet, peaceful	**on pourrait**	we could
chaise longue f	deckchair	**(pouvoir)**	
changer de	to change money	**parasol** m	sunshade/umbrella
l'argent		**parce que**	because
coup de soleil m	sunburn	**passer chercher**	to pick up
crème solaire f	suntan lotion	**plage** f	beach
croire	to believe	**planche à voile** f	surfboard
durer	to last	**pourquoi**	why
faire autre chose	to do something else	**prendre le bateau**	to go by boat
faire une balade	to go for a walk	**retourner**	to return
forêt f	forest	**sable** m	sand
attendre	to wait	**se changer**	to change (clothes)
hall m	hall, lobby	**se faire bronzer**	to lie in the sun
île f	island	**se mettre**	to put on
longtemps	long	**terre** f	the ground, earth
lunettes de	sunglasses	**traversée** f	crossing
soleil f pl		**vague** f	wave
maillot	swim suit/trunks	**visiter**	to visit

The meeting

Day 27 gives you an insight into working life in France. You will learn how to use *ce que* (that/what), and have the opportunity to revise your times and dates. There's also a big vocabulary booster at the end of the chapter.

FURTHER READING…

In order to improve your knowledge of certain areas and industries, it is always helpful to read news articles on a regular basis. These will help you to improve your comprehension skills and vocabulary enormously, and will help you in work and social situations. The French love to discuss current affairs so it is important to keep up to date. Look back to Day 14 on page 145 for more on the French press.

French conversation: Réunion de travail

A l'hôtel au petit déjeuner.

Denis: J'ai préparé une liste. Voilà ce que nous avons à faire au Festival de pub demain et après-demain.

Claire: Le comité d'organisation du Festival m'a envoyé l'ordre du jour détaillé. On l'a déjà lu, les rendez-vous sont déjà fixés. M. Meyer de Munich m'a laissé un message à la réception cet après-midi, il a décalé notre rendez-vous. Je le verrai juste avant de partir.

Denis: Il s'agit de la troisième prise de contact avec lui. Je compte sur toi pour rentrer à Paris avec le contrat en poche !

Claire: Je ne pense pas qu'il se décide aussi vite. Je voudrais faire un rapport au patron, tu m'aideras à le rédiger ?

Denis: Tu peux le préparer et on le relira dans l'avion en rentrant à Paris. Le patron veut un rapport détaillé sur le projet de campagne publicitaire pour la société Meyer qui devrait démarrer en octobre dans la presse spécialisée française.

English conversation: A business meeting

In the hotel during breakfast.

Denis: I've prepared a list. This is what we have to do tomorrow and the day after tomorrow at the advertising festival.

Claire: The festival organizing committee sent me a detailed agenda. We've already read it and the meetings have already been set up. Mr. Meyer from Munich left me a message at the reception desk this afternoon, postponing our meeting. I'll see him shortly before we leave.

Denis: This is the third time we have contacted him. I'm counting on you so that when we return to Paris we'll have a signed contract in our pockets!

Claire: I don't think he will make up his mind that quickly. I'd like to write a report for the boss, will you help me to write it?

Denis: You can prepare it and we'll read through it on the flight back to Paris. The boss wants a detailed account on the planned advertising campaign for the Meyer company, which is set to start in the French trade publications in October.

Grammar

Ce que

The relative pronoun ce que (that) relates to something unspecified; ce que is a direct object pronoun introducing a relative clause. It means 'what' in English.

Voilà tout *ce que* nous avons à faire.	That's all (that) we have to do.
Il fait *ce que* tu veux.	He does what you want.
Voilà *ce que* tu cherches.	That is what you are looking for.

Times and dates

On a rendez-vous *à 9 heures*.	at 9 o'clock
Aujourd'hui c'est *le 28 mai*.	the 28th of May
Le festival de jazz est *en été*.	in the summer
Le festival est *en juillet*.	in July
Le festival est *au mois de juillet*.	in the month of July
Je le rencontre *demain*.	tomorrow
Je le rencontre *demain matin*.	tomorrow morning
Je pars *après-demain*.	the day after tomorrow
Il est parti *hier*.	yesterday
Il est parti *hier après-midi*.	yesterday afternoon
Ils travaillent *toute la journée*.	the whole day
Elle arrive *mardi*.	on Tuesday
Il arrive *samedi matin*.	Saturday morning
J'ai cours *lundi après-midi*.	Monday afternoon
On va au concert *dimanche soir*.	Sunday evening
Qu'est-ce que tu fais *cet après midi* ?	this afternoon
Qu'est-ce que tu fais *ce matin* ?	this morning
Qu'est-ce que tu fais *ce soir* ?	tonight
Je fais du sport *le lundi*.	on Mondays
Elle fait du sport *pendant les vacances*.	during
Je vais en Normandie *à Pâques*.	at Easter
On fait du ski *à Noël*.	at Christmas

Exercises

Exercise 1

Match up the questions on the left with the answers on the right and fill in the blanks.

1 Tu pars quand à Nice ?

2 A .... heure ?

3 Tu restes .... de temps ?

4 Tu rentres .... ?

5 Et mardi tu peux aller au cinéma ?

a Demain ....

b .... 9 heures.

c Tout .... weekend.

d Dimanche .... ou lundi ....

e Non, ... je fais du sport.

Exercise 2

Translate the times in brackets correctly and fill in the blanks.

1 Le Festival du film publicitaire a lieu à Cannes .... (in June).

2 J'ai oublié ce que le patron m'a dit .... (yesterday).

3 Il arrivera en train .... (Friday evening).

4 Nous avons rendez-vous avec Monsieur Meyer .... (tomorrow morning).

5 On préparera la réunion .... (the whole day).

6 Tu as rendez-vous à quelle heure ? .... (at 10 o'clock).

7 Qu'est-ce que tu fais .... (this afternoon)?

8 Je vais à la plage et .... (tonight) au cinéma.

Exercise 3

Complete the text by inserting the appropriate word.

rapport/rendez-vous/campagne/rentrant/qui/en/l'ordre/décaler

J'ai lu .... du jour. Tous nos .... sont fixés, mais notre client allemand a téléphoné pour .... son rendez-vous. J'ai préparé un .... sur le projet de .... publicitaire .... devrait démarrer .... octobre dans la presse. Tu pourrais relire mon texte ? Je le relirai dans l'avion en .... à Paris.

Exercise 4

One word in each line is out of place. Which one?

1	téléphoner	joindre	rappeler	liste
2	ce que	qui	hier	que
3	pendant	agence	firme	société
4	publicité	hôtel	projet	marketing
5	contrat	client	réunion	calme

1.................... 2................. 3................. 4................. 5.................

Exercise 5

Translate the following passage into French:

We have to (il faut que + subjunctive) rearrange all our meetings. Claire will not arrive until (seulement) Monday. She went to Bordeaux over the weekend to see a client.

....

....

....

....

....

....

Vocabulary

Below is a list of vocabulary encountered in this chapter.

aider à	to help with	**laisser**	to leave (behind)
Ascension f	Ascension Day	**liste** f	list
après-demain	the day after tomorrow	**lundi de Pâques** m	Easter Monday
Assomption f	Assumption Day	**lundi de la**	Pentecost Monday
avoir à faire	to have to do/take care of	**Pentecôte** m	
campagne	advertising campaign	**message** m	message
publicitaire f		**Nouvel An** m	New Year
comité	organizing committee	**ordre du jour** m	agenda
d'organisation m		**penser**	to think
compter sur	to count on	**Pentecôte** f	Pentecost
congés payés m pl	paid holiday	**poche** f	pocket
contrat m	contract	**préparer**	to prepare
contrat de	work contract	**presse**	trade publications
travail m		**spécialisée** f	
décaler	to postpone	**prise de contact** f	made contact
demain	tomorrow	**projet** m	project
démarrer	to start	**pub (publicité)** f	advertising
détaillé	detailed	**rapport** m	report
devrait (devoir)	should	**rédiger**	to write
durée f	duration	**relire**	to read through
en poche	in (s.o.'s) pocket	**rendez-vous** m	meeting, date
en rentrant	on the return flight	**réunion de**	business meeting
dans l'avion		**travail** f	
Fête Nationale f	national holiday	**salaire** m	salary
fixé	set (up)	**se décider**	to decide
fonctionnaire m f	civil servant	**service** m	department
grève f	strike	**service du**	personnel department
je le verrai	I will see him	**personnel** m	
(voir)	(to see)	**société** f	company, firm
jour de l'An m	New Year's Day	**Toussaint** f	All Saints Day
jour férié m	public holiday	**vite**	quick, swift

Finding work

Day 28 covers the imperfect tense of *pouvoir* and *vouloir*. This chapter focuses on practising what you have learnt so far, with some additional vocabulary to learn. You will also pick up some more country and culture information about holidays in France.

HOLIDAYS IN FRANCE...

Most French people take a long holiday in July or August. This is peak season as many companies and schools close during the summer. With the exception of the summer holidays, the schools in France take their other annual vacations at different times, depending on which of the three different geographical zones they are in.

French conversation: A la recherche d'un emploi

Dans l'appartement des Rougier rue de Fleurus.

Claire: Je termine mon stage cette semaine à l'agence. Je voulais vous demander si je pouvais rester encore à Paris au mois d'août ?

Caroline: Il faut que je demande à Michel, mais je pense que ça ne pose pas de problème. Je ne serai pas là en août à cause des vacances scolaires. Qu'est-ce que tu comptes faire à Paris en aôut ?

Claire: Je vais chercher du travail. J'aimerais passer une petite annonce dans le journal, j'ai déjà préparé le texte, vous pouvez m'aider pour les abréviations ?

Caroline: D'accord! Montre-moi ton texte: »Jeune fille (J.F.) parlant couramment anglais, allemand, français cherche (ch) emploi temporaire de secrétaire à Paris en août.« Je te conseille de faire passer ton annonce le plus vite possible pour que tu aies une réponse avant la fin du mois de juillet.

English conversation: Looking for a job

In the apartment of the Rougiers family in rue de Fleurus.

Claire: I'll be finishing my internship at the agency this week. I wanted to ask you whether I could stay on in Paris until August.

Caroline: I'll have to ask Michel, but I don't think that it will be a problem. I won't be here in August because of the school holidays. What do you want to do in Paris in August?

Caroline: I am going to look for a job. I want to place a small ad in the newspaper. I've already prepared the text, could you help me with the abbreviations?

Caroline: OK. Show me the text: "Young woman (Jeune fille – J.F.) fluent in English, German, French is looking for (cherche – ch) a temporary job as a secretary in Paris in August". I'd suggest you hand in your ad as quickly as possible so that you get a reply before the end of July.

Grammar

Imperfect tense

pouvoir (to be able to)	vouloir (to want)
je pouvais	je voulais
tu pouvais	tu voulais
il/elle pouvait	il/elle voulait
nous pouvions	nous voulions
vous pouviez	vous vouliez
ils/elles pouvaient	ils/elles voulaient

Perfect and imperfect tense

The perfect tense (see Days 3, 5, 7) is used to convey events and actions of limited duration.
The imperfect tense (see Day 18) is used to describe longer actions, repeated and recurring acts and events in the past.

Compare the following sentences and their tense:

Chez Charrain *je travaillais* beaucoup.
I used to work a lot at Charrain.

Aujourd'hui j'*ai* beaucoup *travaillé*.
I've worked a lot today.

Il *téléphonait* toujours à 8 heures.
He always phoned at 8 o'clock.

Il a téléphoné trois fois aujourd'hui.
He phoned three times today.

Elle *est allée* trois fois à Amsterdam en un an.
She went three times in one year to Amsterdam.

Je *voulais* te téléphoner hier, j'*ai essayé* trois fois.
I wanted to call you yesterday, I tried three times.

Exercises

Exercise 1

Make suggestions using the imperfect tense.

1 Si on (aller) .... aux Etats-Unis cet été ?

2 Si tu (chercher) .... du travail dans un hôtel ?

3 Si vous (rester) .... encore un an à Paris ?

4 Si je (offrir) .... un disque compact à Caroline ?

5 Si tu (passer) .... ton annonce dans deux journaux ?

Exercise 2

Use the perfect tense with être to complete the sentences.

1 Il (arriver) .... à Cannes lundi soir.

2 Nous (aller) .... dimanche à un concert de rock au »Zénith«.

3 Elle (rester) .... six mois dans l'agence.

4 Ils (rentrer) .... en train à Paris.

5 Je (venir) .... en France pour chercher du travail.

Exercise 3

Fill in the perfect and imperfect tense as indicated.

1 Quand Claire (arriver/perfect) .... en France, elle (parler/imperfect) ....
un peu de français.

2 Quand Claire (rencontrer/perfect) .... Denis dans le TGV, elle (chercher/imperfect)
.... du travail.

3 Elle (téléphoner/perfect) .... à l'agence. Elle (dire/perfect) .... qu'elle
(être/imperfect) .... secrétaire.

4 Claire (rencontrer/perfect) .... Abel au Zénith. C' (être/imperfect) .... en
avril.

5 Denis et Claire (louer/perfect) .... une voiture qui (consommer/imperfect) ....
peu d'essence.

6 Ils (téléphoner/perfect) .... à un mécanicien qui (remorquer/perfect) ....
la Clio en panne.

7 Quand Claire (aller/perfect)............... chez le médecin, elle (avoir/imperfect) ....
mal à la tête.

8 Les Rougier (inviter/perfect) .... Claire en Provence. Elle (ne pas connaître/
imperfect) .... cette région.

9 Claire et Miko (aimer/imperfect) .... beaucoup aller aux Puces. Miko (acheter/
perfect) .... des souvenirs.

10 Avant de partir à Cannes, Claire (réserver/perfect) .... deux chambres à l'hôtel qui
(être/imperfect) .... presque complet.

11 A Cannes il (faire/imperfect) .... beau temps, Claire et Denis (aller/perfect) ....
à la plage.

12 Le client de l'agence (oublier/perfect) .... son rendez-vous avec Claire qui
(attendre/imperfect) .... son coup de fil à l'hôtel.

Exercise 4

One word in each line is out of place. Which one?

1 emploi	travail	stage	réponse
2 revenir	retour	rentrer	partir
3 on	SNCF	SVP	CV
4 à propos de	pour	sur	il y a
5 répondre	dire	demander	lire

1 .... **2** .... **3** .... **4** .... **5** ....

Exercise 5

Translate:

I want to place a small ad to find work: "Young woman, fluent in English, French, German, is looking for a temporary job as secretary in Paris in July."

....

....

....

....

....

....

Vocabulary

Below is a list of vocabulary encountered in this chapter.

à cause de	*because, due to*	**problème**	*problem*
à propos de	*regarding, about*	**recherche d'un**	*search for work*
abréviation f	*abbreviation*	**emploi** f	
avoir une réponse	*to get a reply*	**répondre**	*to answer*
compter faire	*to want to do*	**réponse** f	*reply, answer*
conseiller	*to advise*	**retour** m	*return*
décision f	*decision*	**si**	*if, whether*
demander à (qqn)	*to ask (someone)*		*(can also mean yes in*
emploi m	*job*		*answer to a neg. question)*
le plus vite	*as quickly as possible*	**stage** m	*internship*
possible		**temporaire**	*temporary*
montrer	*to show*	**terminer**	*to end*
passer une	*to place an ad*	**texte** m	*text*
annonce		**vacances**	*school holidays*
poser un	*to be problematic/ cause a*	**scolaires** f pl	

Goodbye

Day 29 sees your departure from France. To complete your journey and perfect your French, you will learn the present subjunctive of irregular verbs *avoir, être, aller, faire, venir*. You will then be able to practise what you have learned using the exercises and you will further build your vocabulary.

AIR TRANSPORT...

France is well-connected by air. Paris has two main airports, Charles de Gaulle (you will often hear it being called Roissy also - but don't worry, it's the same airport!), and Orly which is south of Paris. Both of the latter are well-connected by both rail and bus.

Beauvais airport on the other hand is about an hour outside Paris and is only connected by airport bus services.

French conversation: Adieux à l'aéroport

Les passagers du vol BA 308 pour Londre sont priés de se rendre à la porte 3, embarquement immédiat.

Claire:	C'est gentil de m'avoir accompagné à Roissy en R.E.R.
Denis:	Avec la quantité impressionnante de bagages que tu as …
Claire:	J'ai dû payer un supplément pour l'enregistrement !
Denis:	Ça ne m'étonne pas ! La famille et les amis vont crouler sous les cadeaux! Nous sommes en avance mais tu avais tellement peur de rater ton avion. On a largement le temps d'aller prendre un pot avant ton départ.
Claire:	C'est vrai, le vol pour York n'est pas encore affiché. Je voulais te remercier encore une fois pour tout ce que tu as fait pour moi à Paris.
Denis:	Tu exagères ! Tu t'es très bien débrouillée !
Claire:	J'ai invité toute la famille Rougier pour Noël à York. J'aimerais bien que tu viennes me voir avant !
Denis:	Avec plaisir ! J'ai changé ma destination vacances. Je laisse tomber la Guadeloupe.

English conversation: Goodbyes at the airport

(Last call:)	All passengers for flight BA 308 to London, please proceed immediately to gate 3.
Claire:	That's nice of you to accompany me to Roissy on the R.E.R.
Denis:	With that amazing amount of luggage you have …
Claire:	I had to pay a surcharge at the check-in!
Denis:	That doesn't surprise me! Your family and friends are going to collapse under all these presents! We're early but you were so afraid you were going to miss your plane! We have plenty of time to go for a drink before you leave!
Claire:	That's true, the flight to York is not even displayed yet. I'd like to thank you once more for everything you did for me in Paris.
Denis:	You're exaggerating! You looked after yourself very well!
Claire:	I've invited the whole Rougier family to York for Christmas. I would love to see you before that!
Denis:	I'd like that very much! I've changed my holiday destination. I'm not going to Guadeloupe now.

Grammar

Present subjunctive

In French the present subjunctive (**subjonctif**) is used after certain verbs. To refresh what you have already learned on the subjunctive tense, refer back to Day 25.

An example of how the subjunctive is used is:
j'aimerais que tu viennes me voir
I would love it, if you were to visit me (would come to visit me)

The subjunctive must be used in the following cases:

a) after verbs expressing wishes and desires:

aimer que	to love/like to
vouloir que	to want (that)
préférer que	to prefer (that)

The introductory clause and the *que* clause must have different subjects.

b) after **être** + adjective

être content que	to be pleased/happy (that)

c) after impersonal expressions

il faut que	it is necessary, one ought to / must

d) after certain conjunctions

pour que	so as to, so that
avant que	before

e) verbs such as **croire** and **penser** take the subjunctive only if they are in the negative:
Je crois/pense qu'il vient ce soir.
Je ne crois pas/Je ne pense pas qu'il vienne ce soir.

Present subjunctive of irregular verbs

avoir   (to have)

que j'*aie*	que nous *ayons*
que tu *aies*	que vous *ayez*
qu'il/qu'elle *ait*	qu'ils/qu'elles *aient*

être   (to be)

que je *sois*	que nous *soyons*
que tu *sois*	que vous *soyez*
qu'il/qu'elle *soit*	qu'ils/qu'elles *soient*

aller   (to go)

que j'*aille*	que nous *allions*
que tu *ailles*	que vous *alliez*
qu'il/qu'elle *aille*	qu'ils/qu'elles *aillent*

faire   (to do)

que je *fasse*	que nous *fassions*
que tu *fasses*	que vous *fassiez*
qu'il/qu'elle *fasse*	qu'ils/qu'elles *fassent*

venir   (to come)

que je *vienne*	que nous *venions*
que tu *viennes*	que vous *veniez*
qu'il/qu'elle *vienne*	qu'ils/qu'elles *viennent*

Exercises

Exercise 1

Form sentences using the subjunctive of the verbs in brackets, as in the example.

J'aimerais que tu (passer) me chercher à l'hôtel.

J'aimerais que tu passes me chercher à l'hôtel.

1 Je voudrais que tu (faire) .... ton rapport aujourd'hui.

2 Je préfère que tu (venir) . ... me voir à Pâques.

3 Je ne crois pas que tu (être) .... malade.

4 Il aimerait qu'elle (aller) .... avec lui au Japon.

5 On voudrait que les enfants (faire) .... plus de sport cet été.

Exercise 2

Complete the sentences using the subjunctive.

1 Il faut que je (faire) .... un test avant de m'inscrire au cours de langue.

2 Il faut que tu (aller) .... chercher Claire à la gare à 8 heures.

3 Il faut que nous (être) .... à l'aéroport une heure avant le départ.

4 Il faut que vous (venir) .... au Festival du théâtre avec nous.

5 Il faut que tu (chercher) .... son numéro de téléphone.

Exercise 3

Complete the sentences using the subjunctive.

1 Il faut organiser la réunion avant que les clients (arriver) ....

2 J'ai loué une voiture pour que nous (partir) .... en Provence.

3 Il faut qu'elle (parler) .... anglais pour faire ce travail.

4 Il faut que vous (être) .... toute la journée au bureau lundi.

5 On fait les réservations cette semaine pour que vous (avoir) .... les billets d'avion.

Exercise 4

One word in each line is out of place. Which one?

1 R.E.R.	métro	voiture	Noël
2 enregistrement	cadeau	aéroport	bagages
3 Italie	Bavière	Provence	Normandie
4 rentrer	payer	partir	arriver
5 Bavière	Guadeloupe	Provence	Normandie

1 .... **2** .... **3** .... **4** .... **5** ....

Vocabulary

Below is a list of vocabulary encountered in this chapter.

accompagner	*to accompany*	**laisser tomber**	*to let go/fall*
adieux *m pl*	*farewell, goodbye*	**largement**	*sufficiently*
aéroport *m*	*airport*	**Noël** *m*	*Christmas*
aller voir	*to visit*	**passager** *m*	*passenger*
avec plaisir	*with pleasure*	**payer un**	*to pay a surcharge*
avoir le temps de	*to have time to*	**supplément**	
carte	*boarding card*	**porte** *f*	*exit, door*
d'embarquement *f*		**prendre un pot**	*to have a drink (alcholic)*
changer	*to change*	**quantité** *f*	*quantity*
crouler sous	*to break one's back,*	**remercier**	*to thank again*
	collapse under (a weight)	**se débrouiller**	*to look after oneself*
destination *f*	*destination*	**vacances** *f pl*	*vacation*
enregistrement *m*	*check-in*	**vol** *m* **pour**	*flight to*
exagérer	*to exaggerate*		
gentil	*nice*		
impressionnant	*impressive*		
inviter	*to invite*		

day:30

Keeping in touch

Congratulations, you've reached the end of this course! Day 30 tells you how to keep in touch with new friends. You should be confident understanding, speaking, and writing French and should now have a comprehensive vocabulary. Well done!

SOCIAL MEDIA...

The most likely way you'll stay in touch with your new friends will probably be online. Here are some useful sentences to use: **Quel est votre mail ?** *What's your email?;* **Mon mail est...** *My email is...;* **Es-tu sur Facebook/Twitter ?** *Are you on Facebook/Twitter?;* **Quel est ton nom d'utilisateur?** *What's your username?;* **Je t'ajouterai comme ami.** *I'll add you as a friend.;* **Je te suivrai sur Twitter.** *I'll follow you on Twitter;* **Je mettrai les photos sur Facebook/ Twitter.** *I'll put the pictures on Facebook/Twitter.;* **Je te marquerai sur les photos.** *I'll tag you in the pictures.*

French conversation: Cartes postales

Chère Claire,
Je me sens bien seul à l'agence depuis ton départ. C'est une anglaise
qui t'a remplacée. J'en ai assez d'être à Paris et je compte les jours qui nous séparent.
Encore une petite semaine et je retrouverai ton sourire ! Je t'embrasse.
Denis

Chère Claire,
Madame Rougier a fini par me donner ton adresse, mais ça a été dur! Je suis toujours
amoureux de toi, j'attendrai ton retour. Méfie-toi de Denis, j'ai appris qu'il
sort avec la nouvelle stagiaire!
Mille baisers !
Abel

English conversation: Postcards

Dear Claire,
I feel so lonely at the agency since you left. Your have been replaced by an English girl.
I don't want to be in Paris anymore and I am counting the days (that separate us) until
we meet again. Just one more week and I'll see your smile again!
Love,
Denis

Dear Claire,
Mrs. Rougier finally gave me your address but it wasn't easy! I'm still in love with you
and am waiting for you to return. Watch out for Denis, I heard that he's going out with
the new intern.
Lots of love,
Abel

Grammar

Writing correspondance in French

address

Cher ami	(Mon) cher Denis
Chère amie	(Ma) chère Caroline
Chers amis	Chers tous (Dear all)

greetings

amicalement, cordialement	with kind regards
(toutes) nos amitiés	best regards
bons baisers/ grosses bises	lots of love (kisses)
nous vous embrassons/affectueusement	love/love and kisses
en attendant le plaisir de vous lire	looking forward to hearing from you
nous espérons avoir bientôt de vos nouvelles	we look forward to hearing from you soon

Irregular verbs

present tense

aller	faire	pouvoir	vouloir	devoir
je vais	fais	peux	veux	dois
tu vas	fais	peux	veux	dois
il/elle va	fait	peut	veut	doit
nous allons	faisons	pouvons	voulons	devons
vous allez	faites	pouvez	voulez	devez
ils/elles vont	font	peuvent	veulent	doivent

past participle

allé	fait	pu	voulu	dû

present tense

prendre	venir	mettre	avoir	être
je prends	viens	mets	j'ai	suis
tu prends	viens	mets	as	es
il/elle prend	vient	met	a	est
nous prenons	venons	mettons	avons	sommes
vous prenez	venez	mettez	avez	êtes
ils/elles prennent	viennent	mettent	ont	sont

past participle

pris	venu	mis	eu	été

perfect tense + avoir

j'ai pris, tu as pris, il/ elle a pris, nous avons pris, vous avez pris, ils/elles ont pris

perfect tense + être

je suis allé(e), tu es allé(e), il est allé, elle est allée, nous sommes allés/allées, vous êtes allé(e)/ allé(e)s, ils sont allés/ elles sont allées

Note:

perfect tense + être : aller, arriver, venir, entrer, sortir, partir, rester

I was = j'ai été, tu as été etc.

More irregular verbs

		imperfect	future	conditional		
avoir	j'	avais	aurai	aurais	aie	
	tu	avais	auras	aurais	aies	
	il/elle	avait	aura	aurait	ait	
	nous	avions	aurons	aurions	ayons	
	vous	aviez	aurez	auriez	ayez	
	ils/elles	avaient	auront	auraient	aient	
être	j'	étais	serai	serais	sois	
	tu	étais	seras	serais	sois	
	il/elle	était	sera	serait	soit	
	nous	étions	serons	serions	soyons	
	vous	étiez	serez	seriez	soyez	
	ils/elles	étaient	seront	seraient	soient	
aller	j'	allais	irai	irais	aille	
	tu	allais	iras	irais	ailles	
	il/elle	allait	ira	irait	aille	
	nous	allions	irons	irions	allions	
	vous	alliez	irez	iriez	alliez	
	ils/elles	allaient	iront	iraient	aillent	

faire	je	faisais	ferai	ferais	fasse
	tu	faisais	feras	ferais	fasses
	il/elle	faisait	fera	ferait	fasse
	nous	faisions	ferons	ferions	fassions
	vous	faisiez	ferez	feriez	fassiez
	ils/elles	faisaient	feront	feraient	fassent
venir	je	venais	viendrai	viendrais	vienne
	tu	venais	viendras	viendrais	viennes
	il/elle	venait	viendra	viendrait	vienne
	nous	venions	viendrons	viendrions	venions
	vous	veniez	viendrez	viendriez	veniez
	ils/elles	venaient	viendront	viendriont	viennent

Exercises

Exercise 1

Put these verbs into the present tense.

1 Elle (aller) .... travailler tous les jours en métro.

2 Il (pouvoir) .... partir trois semaines en vacances.

3 Nous (devoir) .... rencontrer les Rougier cette semaine.

4 Ils (vouloir) .... apprendre le japonais.

5 Ils (avoir) .... trois enfants.

6 Ils (être) .... tous ingénieurs.

7 Vous (prendre) .... le TGV pour Dijon?

8 Tu (venir) .... avec moi au concert samedi?

9 Ils (faire) .... beaucoup de sport.

10 Elle ne .... (mettre) pas de parfum.

Exercise 2

Rewrite the sentences in the perfect tense.

1 Nous allons souvent aux Etats-Unis.

....

2 Qu'est-ce que tu fais comme sport?

....

3 Il ne peut pas venir en France.

....

4 Elle veut travailler dans le tourisme.

....

5 Je dois partir au Portugal.

....

6 Elle reste à Paris au mois d'août.

....

Exercise 3

Put the following verbs into the present subjunctive.

1 Il faut que vous (faire) .... vos valises avant de partir.

2 Il faut qu'elle (venir) .... ce week-end à Lille.

3 Il faut que nous (aller) .... chercher Claire à la gare.

4 Il ne faut pas que tu (être) .... malade pour mon anniversaire.

5 Il faut que je (avoir) .... tous les documents pour la réunion de travail.

Exercise 4

Give the infinitive of the following verbs.

1 essayé .... allé .... venu ....

pris ....lu ....fini ....

attendu .... parti .... fait ....

mis .... dit ....resté ....

arrivé............................ demandé .... téléphoné ....

Exercise 5

What tense is each verb in?

1 Nous allons souvent aux Etats-Unis.

2 Nous irons aux Etats-Unis en juillet.

3 C'était à Paris en 1995.

4 Je n'ai pas vu Miko aux Puces.

5 Si on allait au cinéma ce soir ?

6 Il faut que tu fasses un rapport détaillé au patron.

7 Je voudrais parler à Monsieur Charrain.

8 Qu'est-ce que tu lui as dit ?

9 Vous étiez aussi au concert samedi ?

10 J'ai pris l'avion à Roissy.

11 Elle a oublié son passeport à l'hôtel.

12 Nous pourrions partir en week-end à Bordeaux.

13 J'ai rendez-vous avec Dominique au restaurant.

14 Elle lit les petites annonces.

15 Vous êtes restés combien de jours à Cannes ?

16 Il faut que tu viennes me voir à York.

present tense: ....

perfect tense: ....

imperfect tense: ....

future tense: ....

conditional tense: ....

subjunctive tense: ....

Exercise 6

Place the nouns according to their gender (masculine = m, feminine = f) in the table below.

magasin/restaurant/gare/aéroport/camping/voiture/ tente/billet/chambre/semaine/ téléphone/rencontre/rendez-vous/journal/agence/anniversaire/panne/essence/ cinéma/client

m ....

....

f ....

....

Exercise 7

Translate the following sentences, then add up your points! (1 point for each correct sentence).

1 I know France well. ....

2 I bought postcards. ....

3 I have no money left. ....

4 It's a quarter to four. ....

5 I speak French. ....

6 He stays in France in Paris. ....

7 She is from York. ....

8 Just keep going straight ahead! ....

9 Turn right! ....

10 We are meeting shortly before 10 o'clock in front of the café.

....

11 I like classical music. ....

12 He is calling him today. ....

13 I am meeting Claire on Saturday. ....

14 He is looking for his ticket. ....

15 I worked the whole day. ....

16 Today is my birthday. ....

Your results

10 to 15 points: .... Félicitations ! (Congratulations!)

8 to 10 points: .... Encore un petit effort ! (Try a little harder!)

7 points or less: .... Une cure de grammaire s'impose ! (You need some grammar help!)

Exercise 8

Imagine you are Claire: Write a postcard to Denis, to Abel or to both of them in response to their letters to you on page 252.

Cher Denis.

....

....

Cher Abel,

....

....

Claire

....

Country and culture quiz

1 If you are invited to a French home you arrive...   **1** ....

   a on time   **b** 15 minutes early   **c** 15 minutes late

2 France is divided into ...   **2** ....

   a arrondissements   **b** départements   **c** nations

3 Saint-Ouen is famous for its...   **3** ....

   a flea market   **b** cheese   **c** cemetry

4 Les Galeries Lafayette is a...   **4** ....

   a Parisian museum   **b** department store in Paris   **c** famous pub in Lyon

5 Le Zénith is a...   **5** ....

   a Parisian concert hall   **b** luxury hotel chain   **c** cigarette brand

6 Le Pariscope is...   **6** ....

   a the nickname for the Eiffel tower   **b** a white wine from Burgundy   **c** an informative magazine covering the cultural scene

7 The TGV is...   **1** ....

   a a stop-and-go commuter train   **b** the French abbreviation for VAT   **c** a high-speed train in France

8 La province is...   **8** ....

   a all of France except Paris   **b** a region in Southern France   **c** a name given to the Parisian suburbs

9 Le Bourgueil is a...   **9** ....

   a famous nightclub   **b** speciality from Provence   **c** famous red wine

10 You leave your luggage at the station with the...   **10** ....

   a consigne   **b** concierge   **c** couchette

11 Le Minitel is   **11** ....

   a a French supermarket chain   **b** an electronic booking system   **c** a short subway line

12 Food stores in France are...   **12** ....

   a open on Sunday mornings   **b** open all day on Sundays   **c** closed on Sundays

13 Les crêpes are a speciality from ...   13 ....

    a Provence   **b** Paris   **c** Brittany

14 La place des Vosges is in ...   14 ....

    a Paris   **b** Grenoble   **c** Cannes

15 The Parisian subway is called ...   15 ....

    a le métro   **b** le R.E.R.   **c** le train

16 If you want to congratulate someone on his or her birthday, you say ...

                                            16 ....

a Bonne fête!   **b** Félicitations!   **c** Bon anniversaire!

17 Le bac is ...   17 ....

    a the driver's licence   **b** the university entrance exam   **c** a sailing permit

18 The French have an apéritif ...   18 ....

    a if they are ill   **b** before meals   **c** after breakfast

19 Les hors-d'oeuvre are ...   19 ....

    a starters/appetizers   **b** desserts   **c** main courses

20 On the 1st of May people give each other as a sign of good luck ...

                                            20 ....

a white chrysanthemums   **b** red tulips   **c** lilies of the valley

21 "A qui sian ben" means ...   21 ....

    a "Goodbye" in Breton   **b** "A good place to be" in   **c** "Cheers" in Catalan

                                  Provençal

22 If you leave a tip for the waiter, you say   22 ....

    a C'est pour vous!   **b** Ça va!   **c** nothing – just leave it on

                                          the table

23 Where do you buy une télécarte?   23 ....

    a à la banqueb   **b** à la poste   **c** aux Puces

24 Un croque-monsieur is ...   24 ....

    a a toasted ham and   **b** the name of a profession   **c** a very young man
       cheese sandwich

Key to Exercises

Day 1

Exercise 1: 1. sont   2. êtes   3. est   4. avez   5. ai   6. êtes
7. suis   8. est   9. ont   10. a
Exercise 2: 1. il   2. elle   3. il   4. elle
Exercise 3: 1. arrive   2. présente   3. présente   4. arrivent
Exercise 4: A. 4   B.1.   C.2.   D.3.
Exercise 5: 1. d   2. c   3. b   4. a

Day 2

Exercise 1: 1. fais   2. va   3. font   4. vais   5. fait   6. va
Exercise 2: de la; du; du; du; des; de la; de la
Exercise 3: des; une; des; des; un
Exercise 4: aime; aime; aimons; aimez; aimes; aiment

Day 3

Exercise 1: prends; prends; prend; prennent; prend; prenons
Exercise 2: 1. Qu'est-ce que vous prenez ?   2. Qu'est-ce que vous aimez faire ?   3. Qu'est-ce que vous voulez faire ?   4. Qu'est-ce que vous faites ?   5. Qu'est-ce que vous prenez ?   6. Qu'est-ce que vous aimez ?   7. Qu'est-ce que vous faites ?   8. Qu'est-ce que vous voulez faire ?
Exercise 3: 1. je dois   2. vous devez   3. elle peut   4. je peux
Exercise 4: 1. d   2. b   3. c   4. a   5. e
Exercise 5: le pain; la gare; les fleurs; les vacances; la ville

Day 4

Exercise 1: 3; 4; 50; 16; 13; 40; 15; 6; 30; 14; 5; 60; 7; 88; 9; 70; 78; 8; 90; 11; 31; 101; 81; 71; 114; 500; 50.000; 3.000; 1.789; 1.918; 1789; 2.000.000
Exercise 2: 1. e mille quatre cent quatre-vingt-douze   2. c mille sept cent quatre-vingt-neuf   3. g mille neuf cent douze   4. h mille neuf cent quarante-cinq   5. f mille neuf cent soixante et un   6. a mille neuf cent quatre-vingt   7. b mille neuf cent quatre-vingt-un   8. d mille neuf cent quatre-vingt-neuf
Exercise 3: j'ai cherché; j'ai accompagné; elle a parlé; elle a aimé; elle a commencé; nous avons téléphoné
Exercise 4: 1. d   2. a   3. c   4. b

Day 5

Exercise 1: on choisit; on va; on téléphone; on attend; on prend; on rentre; on fait
Exercise 2: 1. choisit   2. attendons   3. remplis   4. attendez
5. j'attends
Exercise 3: 1. nous accompagnons   2. ils finissent   3. je travaille
4. on attend   5. elle prend   6. on invite
Exercise 4: 1. j'ai besoin de   2. Bonne fête!   3. on pourrait aller au cinéma!
Exercise 5: le tiroir; la cuisine; la fête; le bois; la surprise; le pain; pour
Exercise 6: 1. m'appelle   2. présente   3. téléphonez
4. demande   5. commence   6. accompagnes   7. rentrez
8. adorent   9. arrives   10. aiment

Test 1

2) 8   4) 20   5) 13   8) 25   12) 16   13) 29   14) 30   16) 22   20) 5   22) 19   25) 14   27)
12   29) 27   30) 4

Day 6

Exercise 1: Est-ce que vous avez une pièce d'identité ?   2. Est-ce que tu rentres tard ?   3. Est-ce que
vous aimez faire du ski ?   4. Est-ce que tu prends le métro ?
5. Est-ce que vous téléphonez à Claire ?   6. Est-ce que vous avez une voiture ?   7. Est-ce que tu peux
passer à la pharmacie ?   8. Est-ce que vous prenez du café au petit déjeuner ?
Exercise 2: 1. je ne prends pas le bus, je prends le métro   2. je ne travaille pas à York, je travaille à
Londres   3. je n'ai pas soif, j'ai faim
faim   4. je ne rentre pas à 5 heures, je rentre à 7 heures   5. je ne commence pas à 9 heures, je commence à 8 heures et demie
6. je n'attends pas Annick, j'attends Florent
Exercise 3: 1. on n'a plus de fruits   2. on n'a plus de sucre   3. on n'a plus de chocolat   4. on n'a plus
de confiture   5. on n'a plus de pain
Exercise 4: 1. e   2. a   3. b   4. f   5. d   6. c
Exercise 5: 1. onze heures moins le quart, on prend un café à la cafétéria   2. midi et quart, je vais
déjeuner avec Caroline   3. deux heures et demie, je passe à la banque   4. trois heures dix, je prends le
métro   5. trois heures vingt-cinq, j'arrive place de l'Odéon   6. trois heures et demie, je rencontre Florent   7. six heures moins le quart, on va au cinéma

Day 7

Exercise 1: Peter Henle est allemand, il vient de Nuremberg, il habite en Allemagne; Bernadette Martial
est française, elle vient de Lyon, elle habite en France; John et Mary Williams sont anglais, ils viennent de

Londres, ils habitent en Angleterre; Lucia Cocci est italienne, elle vient de Florence, elle habite en Italie; José Fernandez est espagnol, il vient de Madrid, il habite en Espagne; Maria Muricy est portugaise, elle vient de Lisbonne, elle habite au Portugal; Sven Johansen est suédois, il vient de Stockholm, il habite en Suède.

Exercise 2:   japonais; anglais; français; allemand; espagnol; italien; suédois; portugais

Exercise 3:   Miko est restée un an à Paris; Peter est rentré à 8 heures; Maria et Carla sont arrivées à Nice; John et Sven sont venus à Versailles; Bernadette et José sont allés à Londres.

Exercise 4:   1. venons   2. arrivons   3. téléphonons   4. cherchons   5. restons   6. visitons
7. déjeunons

Exercise 5:   moderne; Luis; argent; Tokyo

Day 8

Exercise 1:   1. à   2. en   3. à la   4. à la   5. à la   6. en

Exercise 2:   1. à l'   2. au   3. au   4. aux   5. à l'   6. au

Exercise 3:   1. musée   2. États-Unis   3. Espagne   4. place
5. hôtel

Exercise 4:   1. de l'   2. du   3. des   4. de la

Exercise 5:   1. est à New-York aux États-Unis   2. est à Londres en Angleterre   3. est à Madrid en Espagne   4. est à Munich en Allemagne   5. est à Rome en Italie

Exercise 6:   1. a   2. b   3. a   4. a   5. b

Day 9

Exercise 1:   une boîte de thon; deux bouteilles d'eau minérale; une livre de tomates; trois tablettes de chocolat; une litre de lait

Exercise 2:   le thé; l'architecture; le café au lait; les films comiques;
la bière; le vin rouge; les musées

Exercise 3:   je préfère; tu préfères; elle préfère; nous préférons; vous préférez; ils préfèrent

Exercise 4:   1. c   2. d   3. e   4. g   5. f   6. h   7. b   8. a

Exercise 5:   1. Il faut faire les courses.   2. Il faut rentrer à sept heures.
3. Il faut rester un an à Paris.   4. Il faut descendre à Odéon.   5. Il faut téléphoner à l'hôtel.
6. Il faut faire la queue devant le musée.   7. Il faut attendre Claire.
8. Il faut commencer à huit heures.

Exercise 6:   1. peu de   2. beaucoup de   3. trop de
4. deux litres d'   5. trop de   6. peu de   7. assez d'   8. peu de

Exercise 7:   le quartier; le guide; le cours; le Bourgueil

Day 10

Exercise 1: les; la; le; le; l'; le
Exercise 2: ce magasin; ce quartier; ce modèle; cette ville; cet hôtel; cette architecture; cette musique; ce café
Exercise 3: 1. d   2. a   3. e   4. f   5. c   6. b
Exercise 4: bleu; élégante; grises; classique; rouges; verte
Exercise 5: 1. b   2. d   3. f   4. e   5. a   6. c
Exercise 6: 1. c   2. a   3. g   4. b   5. f   6. h   7. e   8. d

Test 2

2) 8   4) 20   5) 13   8) 25   12) 16   13) 29   14) 30   16) 22   20) 5   22) 19   25) 14   27) 12   29) 27   30) 4

Day 11

Exercise 1: yaourts; eau minérale; lait; cigarettes; Are you taking yogurts? Yes, I take six. Is there any mineral water left? Yes, there are three bottles left. Is there any milk left? No, there is none left. Have you got any cigarettes? Yes I still have some.
Exercise 2: 1. c   2. e   3. d   4. a   5. b
Exercise 3: lui; lui; leur; lui; leur
Exercise 4: 1. a   2. b   3. b   4. a   5. b
Exercise 5: le steak; le dessert; le gratin; parler

Day 12

Exercise 1: 1. Prenez-vous le train pour Grenoble ?   2. Allez-vous à Chamrousse ?   3. Prenez-vous un taxi ?   4. Avez-vous un hôtel ?
5. Connaissez-vous ce restaurant ?   6. Faites-vous du ski de fond ?   7. Restez-vous une semaine ?   8. Êtes-vous professeur d'anglais ?
9. Avez-vous un journal ?
Exercise 2: vos; ton; mes; sa; sa; son; sa; mon; ton; leurs
Exercise 3: ma; mes; mon; mon; mes; mon
Exercise 4: 1. ses   2. son   3. son   4. ses   5. sa   6. leur
7. leurs   8. son   9. sa   10. leur   11. sa   12. son
Exercise 5: Je voudrais un billet pour Paris, s'il vous plaît. Aller simple ou aller et retour ? Aller et retour, deuxième classe. Voilà votre billet, vous avez la place 10 dans la voiture 13.   J'arrive à quelle heure ?/A quelle heure est-ce que j'arrive ? A 22 heures.

Day 13

Exercise 1:   1. Le vingt mai, c'est l'anniversaire de Caroline.   2. Le onze novembre, c'est l'anniversaire de Miko.   3. Le huit mars, c'est l'anniversaire de Luis.   4. Le premier avril, c'est l'anniversaire de Claire.   5. Le douze octobre, c'est l'anniversaire de Michel.

Exercise 2:   pars; partez; partons; part; pars; partent

Exercise 3:   1. je me renseigne   2. tu te renseignes   3. vous vous renseignez   4. elle se débrouille   5. il s'appelle   6. les enfants s'amusent

Exercise 4:   1. f   2. d   3. g   4. h   5. c   6. e   7. a   8. b

Exercise 5:   le car; la chambre; coûter; le forfait; août; visiter

Exercise 6:   Pardon, est-ce qu'il y a un car pour les Deux-Alpes ? Il y a un car qui part à 1o heures. Est-ce que vous avez une chambre pour une personne ? Je regrette, tout est complet. Où est-ce que je peux louer des skis ? Est-ce qu'on peut acheter un forfait de ski pour le week-end ?

Day 14

Exercise 1:   lis; lis; achetez; achète; voyez; vois; partons

Exercise 2:   1. C'est Claire qui est assise à côté de Denis.   2. C'est Denis qui travaille dans une agence à Paris.   3. C'est le TGV pour Grenoble qui part à 10 heures.   4. C'est la patronne de l'hôtel qui loue des skis.   5. C'est le restaurant japonais qui n'est pas cher.

Exercise 3:   1. Une chambre à Paris est plus chère qu'une chambre à Chamrousse.   2. Une chambre à Chamrousse est moins chère qu'une chambre à Paris.   3. L'hôtel à Tokyo est plus cher que l'hôtel à Paris.   4. L'hôtel à Paris est moins cher que l'hôtel à Tokyo.   5. L'Europe est plus riche que l'Afrique.   6. L'Afrique est moins riche que l'Europe.   7. La lecture du Figaro est plus facile que la lecture du Monde.   8. La lecture du Monde est moins facile que la lecture du Figaro.

Exercise 4:   est parti; ai rencontré; a acheté; a lu; a vu

Exercise 5:   Je cherche du travail depuis trois semaines. Je lis les petites annonces. J'ai un tuyau pour vous. Mon patron cherche une secrétaire qui parle anglais et allemand. Ça vous intéresse ? Je vous invite demain chez moi à l'apéritif. A quelle heure ? Je travaille jusqu'à sept heures, venez à huit heures.

Day 15

Exercise 1:   1. b   2. b   3. a   4. c

Exercise 2:   2.; 5.; 3.; 6.; 1.; 7.; 4.; 8.; 9.

Exercise 3:   a. 06   b. 13   c. 31   d. 33   e. 34   f. 38   g. 44   h. 51   i. 54   j. 67   k. 69   l. 84

Exercise 4:   1. k   2. b   3. j   4. d   5. l   6. a   7. e   8. c   9. g   10. i   11. h   12. f

Exercise 5:   1. cherchera   2. donnerons   3. parlerez   4. aimeras   5. téléphonerai

Exercise 6:   serai; téléphonera; laisserez; aurai; irai; irons

Exercise 7:   Je ne peux pas déranger M. Charrain. Il est en réunion. Laissez-moi votre numéro de téléphone, s'il vous plaît (s.v.p.). Il vous rappellera à 6 heures.

Exercise 8:   le client; déranger; la société; le voyage d'affaires

Test 3

2) 8   4) 20   5) 13   8) 25   12) 16   13) 29   14) 30   16) 22   20) 5   22) 19   25) 14   27)
12   29) 27   30) 4

Day 16

Exercise 1:   1. toute la journée   2. tous les dossiers   3. tous les candidats   4. tout   5. toutes

Exercise 2:   1. quelle ville   2. quel stage   3. quelle adresse   4. quel journal
5. quels problèmes   6. quelles clés   7. quel rendez-vous   8. quelle annonce

Exercise 3:   1. mets   2. mets   3. met   4. mettez   5. mettent

Exercise 4:   1. tous   2. tous   3. toutes   4. toute
5. tous les étudiants; toutes les étudiantes   6. tous   7. tous
8. toutes   9. tous   10. tout   11. toutes   12. toutes

Exercise 5:   J'ai un rendez-vous demain à 9 heures à l'agence. Je dois écrire un C.V. (curriculum vitae) en français. Je l'écris à l'ordinateur, ça se lit mieux. J'ai fait beaucoup de stages à l'étranger.

Day 17

Exercise 1:   1. Il va être directeur.   2. Elle va organiser la réunion.
3. Je vais manger un steak au poivre.   4. Denis va inviter Claire.
5. Nous allons faire du ski.   6. Je vais acheter les billets.   7. Le car pour Chamrousse va partir.   8. On va prendre un forfait.

Exercise 2:   1. parlera   2. montrera   3. aura   4. sera   5. iront
6. rencontreront   7. ira   8. prendront

Exercise 3:   Je travaille dans une agence de publicité. L'agence est petite mais dynamique. La moyenne d'âge est jeune, l'ambiance décontractée. On a (nous avons) des clients dans toute l'Europe.
En Juin, nous partirons à Cannes.

Exercise 4:   faire; son; sommes; avez; allons

Day 18

Exercise 1:   1. étais   2. arrivait   3. invitions   4. parliez
5. téléphonais   6. était   7. accompagnait   8. aimais

Exercise 2:   1. Si on partait en vacances en Espagne ?   2. Si on prenait le TGV pour Lyon ?   3. Si on faisait des crêpes ?   4. Si on téléphonait à Abel ?   5. Si on louait une voiture ?   6. Si on achetait le Figaro ?   7. Si on invitait Claire dimanche ?   8. Si on discutait de ta candidature ?

Exercise 3: dit; disent; dites; dis

Exercise 4: 1. b   2. a   3. d   4. c

Exercise 5: 3; 10; 9; 1; 2; 7; 8; 4; 6; 5

Exercise 6: 1. c'était un musicien anglais   2. c'était un peintre italien   3. c'était une actrice suédoise   4. c'était un physicien allemand   5. c'était un empereur japonais   6. c'était un acteur français   7. c'était une romancière anglaise   8. c'était un navigateur portugais

Exercise 7: oui; plu; désolé; si; mois

Day 19

Exercise 1: vois; est; ouvre; offrent; a; veulent

Exercise 2: 1. Ils achètent des billets pour aller au concert.   2. On prend un verre de champagne pour fêter l'anniversaire de Denis.
3. Elle téléphone au bureau pour prendre rendez-vous.   4. Je fais un cours de francais pour travailler à Paris.   5. Vous faites un stage de ski pour apprendre à faire du ski.   6. Elles cherchent un hôtel pour rester trois jours à Londres.   7. Je vais aller à la poste pour acheter une télécarte.   8. On prend un kilo de tomates pour faire une salade.

Exercise 3: 1. b   2. c   3. a   4. b

Exercise 4: 1. invitera   2. offrirai   3. offrira   4. ouvrira
5. commencerons   6. mangera   7. retrouvera   8. sera, rentrera

Exercise 5: 1. c   2. a   3. d   4. b   5. f   6. e

Exercise 6: C'est mon anniversaire. Merci beaucoup pour le CD de Miles Davis. Je vous invite au restaurant. Après on pourrait aller danser. La nuit est encore longue !

Day 20

Exercise 1: 1. Laquelle préférez-vous ?   2. Lequel préférez-vous ?
3. Laquelle préférez-vous ?   4. Lequel préférez-vous ?   5. Laquelle préférez-vous ?

Exercise 2: 1. Nous demandons le prix avant de louer une voiture.
2. Nous réservons une chambre avant de partir en week-end.   3. Elle téléphone à Cannes avant d'organiser le voyage d'affaires.   4. Ils achètent les billets avant d'aller au concert.   5. Elles achètent des fleurs avant d'aller chez Luis.

Exercise 3: 1. Si vous allez en voiture à Tours, c'est moins cher.
2. Si vous visitez le Louvre en semaine, c'est plus intéressant.
3. Si tu téléphones à Claire à 8 heures, elle sera là.   4. Si tu rentres à 7 heures, on ira au cinéma.
5. Si nous partons faire du ski, nous réserverons deux chambres.

Exercise 4: 1. b   2. d   3. a   4. e   5. c

Exercise 5: 1. quelle   2. quel   3. quelle   4. quelle   5. quelle
6. quel   7. quel   8. quelles   9. quel   10. quelles   11. quel
12. quels

Exercise 6: 1. Un forfait pour une semaine est plus intéressant qu'un prix à la journée.

2. Les billets de cinéma sont moins chers que les billets de concert.   3. Le japonais est plus difficile que l'anglais.
4. La France est plus grande que l'Italie.   5. Les vacances scolaires en France sont plus longues que les vacances scolaires en Allemagne.
6. Les fromages français sont plus connus que les fromages allemands.   7. Le TGV est plus rapide qu'un train normal.   8. Les hôtels en province sont moins chers que les hôtels à Paris.

Test 4

2) 8   4) 20   5) 13   8) 25   12) 16   13) 29   14) 30   16) 22; 20) 5   22) 19   25) 14   27) 12   29) 27   30) 4

Day 21

Exercise 1:   1. que   2. qui   3. qu'   4. qui   5. que   6. qui   7. qui   8. qui   9. que   10. que
Exercise 2:   1. Claire vient de téléphoner.   2. Vous venez de louer.
3. Ils viennent de passer.   4. Le mécanicien vient de réparer.
5. L'agence vient de rembourser.
Exercise 3:   1. b   2. c   3. a   4. e   5. d
Exercise 4:   1. c   2. b   3. d   4. e   5. a   6. f
Exercise 5: Claire et Denis reviennent de Normandie. Cinquante kilomètres avant Paris ils ont une panne sur l'autoroute. Claire téléphone au service de dépannage. Le mécanicien doit remorquer la voiture.

Day 22

Exercise 1:   1. Elle dit qu'elle a mal à la tête.   2. Elle raconte qu'elle tousse.   3. Elle croit qu'elle a pris froid.   4. Elle dit qu'elle est assurée en Allemagne.   5. Le médecin dit que les frais médicaux sont remboursés.   6. Le médecin dit que la consultation coûte 20 euros.   7. Le médecin dit que Claire a une bronchite.   8. Le médecin dit qu'avec ce temps tout le monde est malade.
Exercise 2:   1. crois   2. crois   3. croyez   4. croyons   5. croit
Exercise 3:   1. b   2. d   3. a   4. c
Exercise 4:   bonjour; facture; repas; par jour
Exercise 5:   Je crois que j'ai pris froid. Vous pouvez me faire une ordonnance pour des antibiotiques ? Prenez ce médicament trois fois par jour. Restez au lit quelques jours. Si ça ne va pas mieux, revenez me voir la semaine prochaine.

Day 23

Exercise 1:   1. Trouvez un appartement en mettant une annonce dans le journal !   2. Perdez 5 kilos en faisant du sport !   3. Montez la tente en arrivant au camping !   4. N'oubliez pas votre lampe de poche en partant !   5. Téléphone à Miko en rentrant à Paris !

Exercise 2: 1. Ils dînent en regardant la télé. 2. Il s'est blessé en montant la tente. 3. Ils ont oublié de payer en partant. 4. Claire a rencontré Denis en allant à Grenoble. 5. Nous avons trouvé le camping en arrivant à Apt.

Exercise 3: 1. arrivés 2. restés 3. venue 4. allés 5. partie

Exercise 4: 1. b 2. d 3. a 4. c

Exercise 5: mai; tarif; saison; gardien

Exercise 6: Nous sommes presque arrivés. Saignon n'est qu'à cinq kilomètres d'Apt. Nous avons /on a de la place pour deux tentes. On monte les tentes. Nous avons /on a oublié la lampe de poche et le marteau.

Day 24

Exercise 1: 1. voyages 2. jours 3. bureaux 4. jeux 5. journaux 6. cadeaux 7. marteaux 8. chapeaux

Exercise 2: 1. Elle n'a pas pris le métro. 2. Il n'a jamais rencontré Abel. 3. Tu n'as plus téléphoné à 11 heures. 4. Elle n'a pas mis de jeans. 5. Je n'ai rien vendu. 6. Elle n'est pas allée à Londres. 7. Nous ne sommes pas arrivés lundi. 8. Tu n'as plus dit bonjour. 9. Je n'ai jamais travaillé le dimanche. 10. Tu n'as pas aimé ce film.

Exercise 3: combien; dommage; soie; glace; grand-mère

Exercise 4: Je voudrais d'abord faire un tour. Essayez ce chapeau! Vous le vendez combien ? C'est trop cher ! Je vais réfléchir.

Day 25

Exercise 1: 1. Il faut que vous organisiez... 2. Il faut que vous téléphoniez... 3. Il faut que vous arriviez... 4. Il faut que vous rencontriez... 5. Il faut que vous travailliez...

Exercise 2: 1. Il faut chercher. 2. Il faut demander. 3. Il faut présenter. 4. Il faut réserver. 5. Il faut penser.

Exercise 3: 1. a 2. b 3. b 4. b

Exercise 4: 1. qui, qui 2. qui 3. que 4. qui 5. qui, que 6. que 7. qu' 8. que 9. qui 10. que 11. que 12. qui

Exercise 5: Allô! Claire Dietz de l'agence Binet, Paris. Je voudrais réserver deux chambres individuelles avec salle de bains du deux au huit mai. Il faut que je confirme ma réservation par email.

Test 5

2) 8 4) 20 5) 13 8) 25 12) 16 13) 29 14) 30 16) 22 20) 5 22) 19 25) 14 27) 12 29) 27 30) 4

Day 26

Exercise 1:   1. pourrions   2. pourrait   3. pourriez   4. pourrais
5. pourrais   6. aimerais   7. aimerais   8. aimeriez   9. aimerions   10. aimerait
Exercise 2:   1. le   2. lui   3. le   4. les   5. l'   6. l'   7. la   8. les   9. leur   10. l'   11. les
Exercise 3:   neige; Paris; eucalyptus; réunion; malade
Exercise 4:   Quel temps fait-il ? Il fait beau, j'aimerais aller à la plage. Moi aussi, mais je dois d'abord
passer/aller à la banque pour changer de l'argent. D'accord, je passe te chercher dans une heure.

Day 27

Exercise 1:   1. a) Demain matin/après-midi/soir.   2. A quelle heure ? b) A 9 heures.
3. combien de temps ? c) Tout le weekend.   4. quand ? d) Dimanche soir ou lundi matin.   5. e) le mardi
Exercise 2:   1. en juin/au mois de juin   2. hier   3. vendredi soir
4. demain matin   5. toute la journée   6. à 10 heures   7. cet après-midi   8. ce soir
Exercise 3:   l'ordre ; rendez-vous; décaler; rapport; campagne; qui; en; rentrant
Exercise 4:   liste; hier; pendant; hôtel; calme
Exercise 5:   Il faut que nous décalions tous nos rendez-vous. Claire arrivera seulement lundi. Elle est
allée le week-end à Bordeaux pour rencontrer/voir un client.

Day 28

Exercise 1:   1. allait   2. cherchais   3. restiez   4. j'offrais   5. passais
Exercise 2:   1. il est arrivé   2. nous sommes allés   3. elle est restée   4. ils sont rentrés   5. je suis
venu/ venue
Exercise 3:   1. est arrivée, parlait   2. a rencontré, cherchait   3. a téléphoné, a dit, était   4. a
rencontré, c'était   5. ont loué, consommait   6. ont téléphoné, a remorqué   7. est allée, avait   8. ont
invité, ne connaissait pas   9. aimaient, a acheté   10. a réservé, était   11. il faisait, sont allés   12. a
oublié, attendait
Exercise 4:   réponse; retour; on; il y a ; lire
Exercise 5:   J'aimerais/ je voudrais passer une petite annonce pour trouver du travail. Jeune femme (J.F.)
parlant couramment anglais, français, allemand cherche (ch) emploi temporaire de secrétaire à Paris en
juillet.

Day 29

Exercise 1:   1. fasses   2. viennes   3. sois   4. aille   5. fassent
Exercise 2:   1. fasse   2. ailles   3. soyons   4. veniez   5. cherches
Exercise 3:   1. arrivent   2. partions   3. parle   4. soyez   5. ayez
Exercise 4:   Noël; cadeau; Italie; payer; Guadeloupe

Exercise 1:   1. va   2. peut   3. devons   4. veulent   5. ont
6. sont   7. prenez   8. viens   9. font   10. met
Exercise 2:   1. sommes allés/allées   2. as fait   3. n'a pas pu
4. a voulu   5. j'ai dû   6. est restée
Exercise 3:   1. fassiez   2. vienne   3. allions   4. sois   5. j'aie
Exercise 4:   1. essayer; aller; venir; prendre; lire; finir; attendre; partir; faire; mettre; dire; rester; arriver;
demander; téléphoner;
2. perfect + être: aller; venir; partir; rester; arriver
Exercise 5:   present: 1./13./14.; perfect: 4./8./10./11./15.; imperfect: 3./5./9.; future: 2.; conditional:
7./12.; subjunctive: 6./16.
Exercise 6:   m: magasin; restaurant; aéroport; camping; billet;
téléphone; rendez-vous; journal; anniversaire; cinéma; client; f: gare; voiture; tente; chambre; semaine;
rencontre; agence; panne; essence
Exercise 7:   1. Je connais bien la France.   2. J'ai acheté des cartes postales.   3. Je n'ai plus
d'argent.   4. Il est/C'est quatre heures moins le quart.   5. Je parle français.   6. Il reste en France
à Paris/ il reste à Paris en France.   7. Elle vient de York.   8. Continuez tout droit.   9. Tournez à
droite!   10. On a/nous avons rendez-vous un peu avant dix heures devant le café.   11. J'aime la
musique classique.   12. Il lui téléphone aujourd'hui.   13. Je rencontre Claire samedi.   14. Il cherche
son billet.   15. J'ai travaillé toute la journée.   16. Aujourd'hui, c'est mon anniversaire./C'est mon anniversaire aujourd'hui.
Exercise 8:   (suggestions)
Cher Denis
Merci pour ta carte. Moi aussi, je me sens bien seule à York depuis mon retour. J'aimerais que tu viennes me
voir bientôt.
Grosses bises.
Claire

Cher Abel
Merci pour ta carte et pour tes informations. Je dois aller à Paris la semaine prochaine. Si tu veux, on pour-
rait se rencontrer à la gare de l'Est. J'arriverai samedi matin à 7 heures moins le quart. Viens me chercher,
on prendra le petit déjeuner ensemble.
Je t'embrasse.
Claire

Country and culture quiz
1. c   2. b   3. a   4. b   5. a   6. c   7. c   8. a   9. c   10. a
11. b   12. a   13. c   14. a   15. b   16. c   17. b   18. b   19. a   20. c   21. b   22. c   23.
b   24. a

Vocabulary refresher

Here is a list of all the vocabulary that you have encountered throughout the book.

A

à	at, to
à 6 heures	at 6 o'clock
à cause de	because of
à côté	around the corner, next door
à droite	to the right
à gauche	to the left
à l'avance	in advance
à la campagne	in the countryside
à la marinière	marinated, pickled
à la place de	instead of
à merveille	wonderful
à part	except
à pied	on foot
à plus tard	until later
à propos de	regarding
À quelle heure ?	At what time?
À ta (votre) santé!	Cheers!
abréviation f	abbreviation
accélérateur m	throttle
accélérer	to accelerate
accent m	accent
accepter	to take, to accept
accompagner	to accompany
accueil m	reception/welcome
acheter	to buy
addition f	bill/check
adieux m pl	farewell
adorer	to enjoy doing
adresse personnelle f	personal address
aéroport m	airport

affaires f pl	things, business
affiché	displayed, posted
afficher	to display
agence de communication f	advertising agency
agneau m	lamb
aider	to assist, help
aider à	to help with
aimer	to like
algérien	Algerian
aller et retour m	return/round-trip ticket
aller simple m	single /one way ticket
aller voir	to go to see, to visit
allons-y	let's go
alors	then
ambiance f	atmosphere/mood
an m	year
année f	year
anniversaire m	birthday
antibiotique m	antibiotics
apéritif m	drink, aperitif
appel m	call
apporter	to bring (along)
approximatif	roughly, approximately
après	after(wards)
après-demain	the day after tomorrow
après-midi	afternoon
architecture f	architecture
argent m	money
arraché	torn
arrivée f	arrival

arriver	to arrive
assez (de)	enough (of)
assistante *f*	assistant f
assuré	insured
attendre (attends)	to wait
au dessus (de)	over
au fait	by the way
au Japon	in Japan
au ski	skiing
aucun(e) idée	not a clue, no idea
aujourd'hui	today
ausculter	to listen to ones chest/breathing
aussi	also, too
autant	as much, as well, like
autoroute *f*	motorway/expressway
autre	other
autre chose	something different; something else
avant de	before
avec plaisir	with pleasure
avion *m*	airplane
avoir ... ans	to be ... years old
avoir à faire	to have to do
avoir besoin de	to need
avoir des frissons	to have fits of shivering
avoir envie (de)	to like to do
avoir faim	to be hungry
avoir le droit	to be allowed
avoir le temps de	to have time to
avoir lieu	to take place
avoir mal à la tête	to have a headache
avoir rendez-vous	to have an appointment
avoir soif	to feel thirsty
avoir une idée de	to have an idea of
avoir une réponse	to get a reply

B

bac *m*	school leaving exams
bagages *m pl*	luggage
balade *f*	walk, stroll
banlieue *f*	suburb
bas-côté *m*	(road) shoulder
beaucoup (de)	much, plenty, a lot of
belge	from Belgium
ben	well yeah (colloquial)
beurre *m*	butter
bien	well
bien sûr	of course, obviously
bienvenue *f*	welcome
bière *f*	beer
bilingue	bilingual
billet *m*	ticket
billet d'avion *m*	airplane ticket
bise *f*	kiss
bœuf *m*	beef
boisson *f*	drink
boîte *f*	nightclub
bon adv.	well
bon, bonne adj.	good
Bon anniversaire !	Happy birthday!
Bonjour!	Hello!
Bonne chance !	Good luck!
Bonne fête !	All the best on your name day!
bonnet *m*	cap, hat
borne téléphonique *f*	emergency phone
botte *f*	boot
bourse *f*	scholarship
bronchite *f*	bronchitis
bruit *m*	noise, sound
bureau *m*	office
bus *m*	city bus

C

C.V. (cévé) *m*	CV (Curriculum Vitae)
C'est à quel sujet ?	About what?
c'est exact	that's correct
c'est gentil	that's nice
c'est tout	that's all
ça	that
ça sera tout	that's all
ça t'ennuie si …?	would you mind if…?
Ça va ? (aller)	Is it okay?/How are you?
Ça vous plaît ?	Do you like it?
Ça vous va ?	Does that suit?/ Is it alright?
cabine d'essayage *f*	dressing room
cachet *m*	tablet, pill
cadeau *m*	gift, present
café *m*	coffee
café au lait *m*	coffee with milk (at home)
(café) crème *m*	coffe with milk (at a café)
cafétéria *f*	cafeteria
calendrier *m*	diary /schedule, calendar
calme	calm, quiet, peaceful
campagne *f*	countryside
campagne publicitaire *f*	advertising campaign
camping *m*	camping
camping-gaz *m*	camping stove
candidature *f*	application
car *m*	coach, long distance bus
carotte *f*	carrot
carte d'embarquement *f*	boarding pass
carte de crédit *f*	credit card
carte de visite *f*	(business) card
carte *f*	menu
caution *f*	deposit
ce/cet/cette/ce que	this/that/what

ce que	what, which
ce soir	tonight, this evening
célibataire	single (not married)
celui de	that at
centre ville	city centre/downtown
ces	these/those
c'est moi	that's me
cet après-midi	this afternoon
cette année	this year
chacun(e)	each, everyone
chaise longue *f*	deckchair
chaleur *f*	heat
chambre (d'hôtel) *f*	(hotel) room
chambre individuelle *f*	single room
chambre pour deux personnes *f*	double room
champ de lavande *m*	lavender field
chance *f*	luck
changer	to change
chapeau *m*	hat
chaussette *f*	sock
chaussure *f*	shoe
chef-d'œuvre *m*	masterpiece
chemise *f*	shirt
chemisier *m*	blouse
chèque *m*	cheque
chez moi	at home, at my place
chocolat *m*	chocolate
choisir	to choose
choix *m*	choice
chute de neige *f*	snowfall
ciné *m* (colloquial for cinéma)	cinema
citron *m*	lemon
citron vert *m*	lime

classique	classic(al)
client m	client, customer
colin m	hake
collant m	a pair of tights
collègue m/f	colleague
combien de	how many
comme	how, as, like
commencer	to start
comment	like, how
complet	fully booked (up), sold out
complètement	completely
composter	(here:) to stamp/validate
compris	inclusive
compter faire	to want to do
compter sur	to count on
concert m	concert
condition f	condition, term
conducteur m	(car) driver
confirmer	to confirm
confiture f	jam /marmalade Am
congés payés m pl	paid holiday
connaître	to know
connu	well-known
conseiller à/de	to advise (to)
conservatoire m	(music) academy
consigne f	left luggage
consommer	to consume
consultation f	consultation
contact m	contact
continuer	to continue
contrat m	contract
contrat de travail m	work contract
convenir	to like
copain m	friend (male)
copine f	friend (female)
correspondance f	connection

correspondant	accordingly
corriger	to correct
côté cour	facing the back (yard)
coton m	cotton
couchette f	bunk, berth
couleur f	colour
couloir m	corridor
coup de soleil m	sunburn
coupe de cheveux	haircut
couramment	fluent
courant	fluent(ly)
cours de français m	French course
cours de langue m	language course
cours intensif m	intensive course
cours moyen m	intermediate level
court	short
coûter	to cost
crème solaire f	suntan lotion
crêpe f	crêpe, pancake
crevette f	shrimp
cric m	jack (for a car)
crois (croire)	to believe
croque-monsieur m	toasted ham and cheese sandwich
crouler sous	to collapse under (a weight)
cuillère f	spoon
cuillerée f	a spoonful
cuir m	leather
cuisine f	kitchen

D

d'abord	first
d'accord	agreed, OK
d'habitude	normally
dans	in

dans ce cas	in that case
dans l'avion	flight
de bonne heure	early in the day
de toute façon	anyway, in any case
décaler	to postpone
décider	to decide
décision f	decision
décontracté	relaxed
décousu	undone, unstitched
découvert (découvrir)	discovered
découverte f	discovery
déjà	already
demain	tomorrow
demain matin	tomorrow morning
demain soir	tomorrow evening
demander à	to ask
démarrer	to start up, pull away
dépanneuse f	tow truck
départ m	departure
depuis	since
déranger	to interrupt, disturb
dernier	last
des cours m	program
descendre	to exit
désirer (désirez)	to want, desire, like
désolé(e)	I'm sorry/ regrettably
dessert m	dessert
destination f	destination
détaillé	in detail
deuxième classe	second class
devenir	to become
devoir (vous devez)	to have to, must
devoirs m pl	homework
devrait (devoir)	should

dictionnaire m	dictionary
difficile	difficult
dîner	to dine, to eat dinner
dîner m	dinner
dire (dis)	to say
directeur m	director, manager
direction f	direction
discuter de	to discuss
disque compact m	CD
dit (dire)	said
divorce m	divorce
divorcé(e)	divorced
Dommage!	What a pity!
donner	to give
dormi (dormir)	slept
douleur f	pain
drôle	funny, odd
du moins	at least
durée f	duration
durer	to last
dynamique	dynamic

E

eau minérale f	mineral water
échanger	to exchange
échangeur m	intersection
écharpe f	scarf
écouter	to hear
écrit (écrire)	written
élégant	elegant
emmener	to take along
emplacement tente m	camping site
emploi m	job
employé m	employee
en automne	in the autumn

en bas	below, down	essence f	petrol /gas
en bois	(made) of wood	essuie-glace m	windscreen /windshield
en ce moment	at the moment		wiper
en codes m pl	with dipped /dimmed	est (être)	is
	headlights	Et toi ?	And you?
en coton	made of cotton	étagère f	shelf
en détail	in detail	était (être)	was (to be)
en espèces	in cash	état civil m	marital status
en été	in the summer	étonnant	surprising
en français	in French	étranger	foreign
en France	in France	étranger m	abroad
en hiver	in the winter	être à la	to be available to
en partant	when you leave	disposition de	
en plastique	(made) of plastic	être à la journée	good for one day
en plus	in addition, besides	être assis	to sit
en poche	in (s.o.'s) pocket	être au niveau	to be at that level
en rentrant	on the return	être dans la direction	to be in the direction
en semaine	during the week	étroit	tight
en tout	in total	études f pl	studies
encore	still	étudiant(e) m(f)	student
enfant m	child	eu (avoir)	had (to have)
enregistrement m	check-in	eucalyptus m	eucalyptus
ensemble	together	évaluation f	assessment
entendre	to hear	événement m	event
entendu	all right, of course	évier m	sink
entouré de	surrounded by	exagérer	to exaggerate
entre	between	examiner	to examine
entrée f	starter, appetizer	excellent	excellent
entreprise f	company, business	exercice à	multiple choice exercise
entretien m	conversation	choix multiple	
environ	approximately, about	expérience f	experience
envoyer	to send	express m	espresso
escalier m	staircase, stairs	extraordinaire	great, extraordinairy
essai m	try/attempt		
essayer	to try out/on		

F

facile	*easy*
facture *f*	*invoice*
fait (faire)	*done*
faire	*(here:) to offer*
faire autre chose	*to do something else*
faire de la randonnée	*to hike*
faire demi-tour	*to turn around*
faire des études	*to study*
faire des photos	*to take photos*
faire du camping	*to camp*
faire du ski	*to ski*
faire du vélo	*to cycle*
faire l'affaire	*to do it as well*
faire la cuisine	*to cook*
faire la queue	*to stand in line*
faire le plein	*fill the tank*
faire les courses	*to go shopping*
faire partie de	*to be a part of something*
faire un tour	*to look around*
faire une balade	*to go for a walk*
faire une ordonnance	*to write a prescription*
famille *f*	*family*
fatigué	*tired*
Félicitations! *f pl*	*Congratulations!*
femme *f*	*woman, wife*
fenêtre *f*	*window*
fenouil *m*	*fennel*
fermé	*closed*
fête *f*	*name day*
Fête Nationale *f*	*national holiday*
fêter	*to celebrate*
film *m*	*film, movie*
fin *f*	*end*
finir	*to end, to finish*
fixé	*set (up)*

fleur *f*	*flower*
fleurir	*to bloom*
fois *f*	*times*
fonctionnaire *m f*	*civil servant*
forêt *f*	*forest*
forfait *m*	*ski-pass/flat rate*
formation *f*	*training*
fort	*strong*
foulard *m*	*scarf*
frais de réparation *m pl*	*repair costs*
frais médicaux *m pl*	*medical costs*
frais pharma- ceutiques *m pl*	*cost for medications*
français(e)	*French, from France*
frein *m*	*brake*
freiner	*to brake*
frisée *f*	*frisee lettuce*
froid *m*	*cold*
fromage *m*	*cheese*
fruit *m*	*fruit*
fruits de mer *m pl*	*seafood*
fumer	*to smoke*
fumeur *m*	*smoker*

G

gant *m*	*glove*
garage *m*	*garage*
gardien (du camping) *m*	*guard, administrator*
gare *f*	*station*
généraliste *m*	*general practitioner*
génial	*great, super*
gentil	*nice*
glace *f*	*ice cream, mirror*
goûter *m*	*snack (for children)*

grammaire f	grammar
grand	large, big
grand magasin m	department store
grandes lignes f pl	long distance journeys
grand-mère f	grandmother
grand-père m	grandfather
gratin dauphinois m	potatoes au gratin
grève f	strike
gros	fat, big
gruyère m	gruyère cheese
guichet m	ticket counter
guide m	guide

H

habiter	to live, stay
hall m	entrance hall, lobby
haricot m	bean
Hein ?	Isn't it?/OK?
hésiter	to hesitate
heure f	time (of day)
heures de consultation f pl	consultation hours
heureusement	luckily
hier	yesterday
horaire m	timetable, (here:) per hour
hors-d'œuvre m	(cold) starter /appetizer Am
huître f	oyster

I

ici	here
idée f	idea
il est	it is
il fait un temps ...	it is ... weather
il faut (falloir)	one must, one has to
il s'agit de (s'agir de)	it is about/has to do with

il y a (une semaine)	(one week) ago
île f	island
illimité	unlimited
immense	immense, huge
imperméable m	raincoat
important	important
impression f	impression
impressionnant	impressive
informaticien m	IT specialist
inscription f	enrolment
inscrire	to enroll
inspecter	to inspect
instant m	moment
intéressant	interesting
intéresser	to interest
inviter	to invite

J

j'aimerais (aimer)	I would like
japonais(e)	Japanese, from Japan
jardin m	garden
je le verrai (voir)	I will see him
je m'appelle (s'appeler)	I'm called/named
je mettrais	I would write
je suis	I am
je te présente	I introduce to you
je voudrais	I would like
jean m	jeans
jeudi prochain	next Thursday
jeune	young
jeune homme m	young man
joindre	to add, attach/enclose
jour de l'An m	New Year's Day
jour férié m	public holiday
journal m	newspaper

journée f	day
Joyeux anniversaire !	Happy birthday!
jupe f	skirt
jus de fruits m	fruit juice
jusqu'à	up to, until
juste	only

K

kilo m	kilogram
kilométrage m	mileage
klaxonner	to honk/beep

L

l'Angleterre f	England
l'Argentine f	Argentina
la classe	stylish
la dernière fois	the last time
la France	France
la prochaine	the next
la semaine prochaine	next week
la voiture est garée	the car is parked
lac m	lake
laisser	to let, leave behind
laisser tomber	to let go/fall
laitue f	lettuce
lampe de poche	flashlight
langue maternelle m	native language
large	wide, baggy
largement	sufficiently
le Japon	Japan
le matin	in the morning
le plus vite possible	as quickly as possible
lecture f	reading
légume m	vegetable
les dernières vacances	the last vacation

les Puces f pl	flea market
libre	free
lion m	lion
liquide	cash
lire	to read
lisible	legible
liste f	list
location f	rental
loin	far (away)
Londres	London
long/longue	long
longtemps	long (time)
louer	to hire /rent
loup de mer m	sea bass
lu (lire)	read
lundi de Pâques m	Easter Monday
lunettes de soleil f pl	sunglasses
lycée m	high school

M

Madame f	Mrs./Ms.
Mademoiselle f	Miss/Ms.
maillot (de bain) m	swim suit/trunks
mais	but
malade	sick, ill
malade m/f	ill person
Mamie	grandma
manger	to eat
manteau m	coat
manuscrit	handwritten
marchand (de légumes) m	vegetable merchant
marché m	market
marcher	to walk
mari m	husband
mariage m	marriage

marié(e)	married
marteau *m*	hammer
matériel *m*	gear, equipment
maternelle *f*	kindergarten
mécanicien *m*	mechanic
médecin *m*	GP /doctor
médicament *m*	medicine
meilleur	better
même	(the) same
mentionner	to specify, mention
menu *m*	set menu
merci	thank you
message *m*	message
Messieurs Dames	ladies and gentlemen
météo *f*	weather report
métro *m*	underground /subway Am
mettre	to list, specify
mieux	better
modèle *m*	model
moderne	modern
moi aussi	me too
mois *m*	month
monastère *m*	monastery
moniteur (de ski) *m*	(skiing) instructor
Monsieur *m*	Mr.
monter une tente	to pitch a tent
montrer (à)	to show (to)
moule *f*	mussel
moyenne d'âge *f*	average age
musée *m*	museum
musique *f*	music

N

nager	to swim
nationalité *f*	nationality
Ne vous en faites pas!	Don't worry!

né(e)	born
ne ... rien	nothing
neige *f*	snow
niveau *m*	level
niveau avancé *m*	advanced level
niveau moyen *m*	intermediate level
Noël *m*	Christmas
non-fumeur	non-smoking
normal	normal
nouveau/nouvel	new
Nouvel An *m*	New Year
nuit *f*	night
numéro de téléphone *m*	telephone number

O

offert par la maison	on the house
offrir	to give
omelette *f*	omelet
on dirait (dire)	it seems
on pourrait (pouvoir)	one/we could
on voulait (vouloir)	we wanted
opéra *m*	opera house
opposé	opposite
oral	orally
ordinateur *m*	computer
ordonnance *f*	prescription
ordre du jour *m*	agenda
organisation *f*	structure, organization
organiser	to organize
oser	to dare
Où ?	Where?
ouais (coll. for oui)	yes, yeah
oublier	to forget
ouvrir	to open (up)

P

pain *m*	bread
panne *f*	breakdown
pantalon *m*	a pair of trousers /pants
Pâques *m*	Easter
par fax	by fax
par jour	daily
par là	in this direction
par personne	per person
parasol *m*	sunshade/parasol
parce que	because
pardon	excuse me
parents *m pl*	parents
parfait	perfect, great
parlé et écrit	written and spoken
parler à	to talk with/to
parler de	to speak about
partager	to share
partie *f*	part
pas *m*	footstep
pas bien	probably not
pas cher	not expensive
pas de problème	no problem
pas du tout	not at all
pas encore	not yet
pas mal	not bad
passager *m*	passenger
passeport *m*	passport
passer	to run, play (a movie), appear on stage, pass (by)
passer à	to go (to)
passer chercher	to pick up
passer un test	to take a test
passer une annonce	to place an ad
patron *m*	boss

payer	to pay
pays *m*	country
penser (à)	to think (of)
permettre	to allow, permit, let
permis de conduire *m*	driving licence
petit	small, little
petit pois *m*	pea
petites annonces *f pl*	classified (small) ads
peut-être	maybe
phares *m pl*	lights/headlights
pharmacie *f*	chemist's /pharmacy
pharmacien *m*	chemist /pharmacist
photo *f*	photo
pièce *f*	piece
pièce d'identité *f*	form of ID
pierre *f*	stone
pintade *f*	guinea fowl
piquet *m*	tent peg
piqûre *f*	syringe, injection
piscine *f*	swimming pool
piste *f*	ski run/slope
placard *m*	cupboard
place (assise) *f*	seat (seating place)
place *f*	square
plage *f*	beach
plan *m*	street plan/map
planche à voile *f*	surfboard
planter	to insert
pleine saison *f*	peak season
pleins phares	high beam
plongé dans	absorbed in
plu (plaire)	to enjoy/like
plus cher	more expensive
plus du tout	nothing any more
plus simple	more simply
plus tard	later

pneu *m*	tyre /tire
pneu à plat *m*	flat tyre /tire
poche *f*	pocket
pointure *f*	shoe size
poisson *m*	fish
poivre *m*	pepper
pomme *f*	apple
pomme de terre *f*	potato
porc *m*	pork
porte *f*	exit
poser sa candidature	to apply for (a job)
poser un problème	to be problematic
possible	possible
poulet *m*	chicken
pour	for
pourquoi	why
pourquoi pas	why not
pouvoir (vous pouvez)	to be able to, can
préciser	to mention
préférer	to prefer
premier	first
première classe	first class
prendre (vous prenez)	to take
prendre froid	to catch a cold
prendre le bateau	to go by boat
prendre un pot	to have a drink
préparer	to prepare
près de	close to
prescrire	to write a prescription
présenter	to introduce
presque	quick
presse	trade
prévoir (prévoit)	to forecast/predict
prise de contact *f*	made contact
prix *m*	price

problème *m*	problem
prochain	next
prof m	teacher (colloquial)
professeur *m*	teacher
professionnel	professional
profiter de	to enjoy
programme *m*	programme
programme des cours	programme of courses / course catalog/catalogue
projet *m*	project
promis (promettre)	promised
proposer	to suggest
provençal	from Provence
publicitaire	advertisement
publicité (pub) *f*	advertising
pull *m*	sweater

Q

Qu'est-ce que ?	What?
Qu'est-ce que vous faites dans la vie ?	What do you do for a living?
quai *m*	platform
qualité *f*	quality
quand	when, whenever
quand même	nevertheless, despite, as well
quantité *f*	quantity
quart d'heure *m*	quarter of an hour/15 minutes
quartier *m*	neighborhood/ neighbourhood
Quelle chaleur!	It's hot!
Quelle galère!	What a nuisance!
quelqu'un	someone
quelque chose	something
question *f*	question
qui	who/which/that
quoi	what

R

raconter	to tell, narrate
ralentir	to slow down
ramener	to return
randonnée f	hike
rappel de limitation	traffic sign
rappeler	to call back (on the phone)
rapport m	report
rayon m	section, department
réceptionniste f	receptionist
recherche d'un emploi f	search for work
recommander à	to recommend to
rédiger	to write
réfléchi (réfléchir)	thought
réfléchir	to think, reflect on
regard m	look, view
regarder	to look up, check
régional	regional
régler	to pay
rejoindre	to join
relire	to read through
remboursement m	reimbursement
rembourser	to reimburse
remercier	to thank again
remontée mécanique f	ski lift
remorquer	to tow
rencontre f	meeting, encounter
rencontre professionnelle f	business meeting
rencontrer	to meet, to get to know
rendez-vous m	meeting, appointment
rendre	to hand in, return to
rentrer	to return
rentrer du	to return from

réparer	to repair
repartir	to fly back, return
repas m	meal, food
répondre	to answer
réponse f	reply, answer
réservation f	reservation
réserver	to reserve, to book
réservoir d'essence m	petrol /gas tank
ressembler à	to have in common/look like
restaurant m	restaurant
rester	to remain, to stay
rester au lit	to stay in bed
résultat m	result
retour m	return /roundtrip
retourner	to return
retrouver	to meet
réunion f	meeting
réunion de travail f	business meeting
revenir	to return, go back
revenir de	to return (from)
rez-de-chaussée m	ground floor
rien de prévu	nothing planned
ringard	old fashioned
roi m	king
rôti m	roast
rouge	red
rue f	street

S

s'allonger	to lie down
s'amuser	to have fun
s'approcher de	to approach someone
s'arrêter	to stop oneself
s'il vous plaît, s.v.p. (abbrv.)	please
s'installer	to settle down

s'occuper de	to take care of	sérieux	serious
sable m	sand	service de cars m	bus connection
sac m	(travel) bag	service m	favour, department
sac (à main) m	handbag, backpack	service de	road service
sac de couchage m	sleeping bag	dépannage m	
saison f	season	service du	personnel department
salade f	salad, lettuce	personnel m	
salade composée f	mixed salad	servir à (sers)	to serve, bring, get
salade de fruits f	fruit salad	seulement	only
saladier m	bowl	si	if/whether/in case, in spite
salaire m	salary		yes (in answer to a negative
salle f	room		question)
salle de bains f	bath(room)	si possible	if possible
salut	hello	simple	simple, easy
sandwich m	sandwich	sirop m	cough syrup
sanitaires f pl	bathrooms	ski m	skiing
sans plomb	unleaded	ski alpin m	downhill skiing
saucisson m	salami	ski de fond m	cross country skiing
savoir	to be able, know how	SNCF f	French state-run railway
savoir (sais)	to know	société f	company, firm
se changer	to change (clothes)	soir m	evening
se débrouiller	to get by, look after oneself	soirée f	evening
se décider	to decide	soleil m	sun
se dépêcher	to hurry up	sortie (d'autoroute) f	exit on a motorway /
se déshabiller	to get undressed		highway Am
se mettre	to put on	sortir (de)	to leave
se présenter	to introduce oneself	soupe f	soup
se servir (servez-	to help oneself	sous	underneath
vous)		sous forme de	in the form of
se tromper	to be mistaken	souvent	often
séance f	showing	spécialiste m	specialist (doctor)
sec	dry	spécialité f	speciality
secrétaire f	secretary	spectateur m	spectator
semaine f	week	splendide	wonderful
sens interdit	no entry (sign)	sport m	sport
sens unique	one-way street	stage m	course, internship

stagiaire m/f	trainee, intern
station f	train station
steak m	steak
style m	style
sucre m	sugar
sucrer	to sprinkle with sugar
suivre (suivez)	to join/to follow
super	super
superbe	very nice, great
supplément m	surcharge
sûr	certain, sure
sur moi	with me
surprise f	surprise
sympa	nice

T

table f	table
taille f	size
taper sur ordinateur	to type on the computer
tard	late
tarif m	price
tarte f	fruit tart
téléphoner à	to phone
temporaire	temporary
tente f	tent
tenter	to try
terminer	to end
terrain de camping m	camping site
test m	test
texte m	text
thé m	tea
théâtre m	theatre
tiens (tenir)	here (take)
tiroir m	drawer
tissu m	fabric, material
tomate f	tomato

tomber	to fall
tôt	early
toujours	always
tourner	to turn round
tous	all
tous les jours	every day
Toussaint f	All Saints Day
tousser	to cough
tout	all
tout de suite	immediately
tout droit	straight ahead
tout l'après-midi	the entire afternoon
tout le monde	all, everybody
tout près de	very close to
toutes (f pl)	all
toutes directions	all directions
toutes les deux f pl	both
toutes les heures	every hour
toutes taxes comprises (T.T.C.)	all-inclusive
train m	train
train corail m	(train with) open carriage
trains de banlieue m pl	commuter trains
travail m	work, job
travailler	to process, to work
traversée f	crossing
très	very
très bien	very good
trop de	too much (of)
trouver	to find, discover
tu pourrais (pouvoir)	you could (informal)
Tu pourrais … ?	Could you … ?
tulipe f	tulip
tutoyer (tutoie)	to address with the familiar "tu"
tuyau m	tip, hint

U

un peu	a little
uniquement	only
Uuf !	Phew!

V

vacances f pl	vacation
vague f	wave
valise f	suitcase
vélo m	bicycle
vendeur m	vendor, seller
vendredi	Friday
venir (viens)	to come
venir de faire	to have just done something
verre m	glass
vers	at about, against,
vert m	(color) green
veste f	jacket
veuf, veuve	widowed
viande f	meat
vie f	life
vieux	old
village m	village
ville f	city, town
vin m	wine
vin blanc m	white wine
visite guidée f	guided tour
visiter	to visit
vite	quick, swift
vitesse f	speed

voie f	track
voilà	well then
voiture de location f	rental car
voiture f	car, train carriage
voix f	voice
vol m	flight
vol aller m	outgoing flight
vol m pour	flight to
vol retour m	return flight
votre	your (formal)
vouloir	to want
vouloir (je voudrais, vous voulez)	to want to
vous êtes	you are
Vous êtes libre ?	Are you free?
vous pourriez (pouvoir)	you could (formal)
voyage d'affaires m	business trip
vraiment	actually/really

W

wagon-lit m	sleeper car
wagon-restaurant m	dining car, restaurant
week-end m	weekend

Y

| yaourt m | yogurt |

Z

| Zut ! | Damn! |